PRAISE FOR CAREER

"Anyone who wants to fast trac
book."
Andrew Stembridge, Managing Director, Chewton Glen

"Like all the best products, this book does exactly what it says
on the tin. Contained within its pages are secrets that will make
sales people more successful, leaders more effective, and give
owner managers a distinct advantage over their competitors.
Buy it. Read it. Live it"
Dan Collins, Founder, Fresh Group

"*Career Helium* is the *Who Moved My Cheese* for the 21st
century. A great read."
Samantha Allen, Managing Partner, Consumer & Retail,
Whitehead Mann

"As a CEO, I found the advice contained within *Career Helium*
to be useful, practical, and achievable by anyone with career
advancement aspirations."
David J. DiStefano, President & CEO, Richardson

"One of the many great things about this book is that it explains
that you don't have to walk over people to get on. That's
refreshing."
Danny Pecorelli, Managing Director, Exclusive Hotels

CAREER HELIUM

CAREER HELIUM

HOW TO FLOAT PAST OTHERS IN YOUR QUEST TO REACH THE TOP

DAVID THOMPSON

Carly –

Hope that you enjoy this!

Thanks for all your help!

12-8-10

CYAN

mc Marshall Cavendish
Business

Copyright © 2007 David Thompson

First published in 2007 by:

Marshall Cavendish Limited
119 Wardour Street
London W1F 0UW
United Kingdom
T: +44 (0)20 7565 6000
F: +44 (0)20 7734 6221
E: sales@marshallcavendish.co.uk
www.marshallcavendish.co.uk

and

Cyan Communications Limited
119 Wardour Street
London W1F 0UW
United Kingdom
T: +44 (0)20 7565 6120
F: +44 (0)20 7565 6121
E: sales@cyanbooks.com
www.cyanbooks.com

A CIP record for this book is available from the British Library

ISBN-13 978-0-462-09900-2
ISBN-10 0-462-09900-8

Designed and typeset by Phoenix Photosetting,
Lordswood, Chatham, Kent

Printed and bound in Great Britain by
TJ International Ltd, Padstow, Cornwall

For Dax

Matt watched himself enter the elevator. The door closed slowly and his eyes drifted toward the numbers counting up above the silver door. 24, 25, 28, 33, 38, 52, 74. The flickering numbers took larger and larger jumps. Matt felt a strange sensation—pressure against his chest and face.

"We're rising, my friend," said a voice behind him. Matt hadn't been aware of anyone in the elevator with him until the point he heard the man's haunting voice.

He saw himself turn round to see an old man standing in the corner, holding tightly onto the hand rail that wrapped around the inside of the elevator.

The old man's eyes flicked between Matt and the numbers above the door—138, 165, 180. The numbers dimmed as the ceiling of the elevator turned to clear glass and sunlight shone brightly onto the display.

Shooting through the lift shaft like a bullet in a gun, Matt screamed as he was jolted to the floor. The elevator shuddered with the force of the blast that shot it through the roof of the building and into the open air above, ploughing through the sky like a rocket toward the stars.

"Higher and higher and higher," said the voice behind him. Matt ignored the voice until the old man caught his attention:

"Onwards and upwards, Matt." The mention of his name from this man that he had never met sent a shiver through his entire body.

"It's another beautiful day—the time is exactly 7.24 AM, and here's a favorite to get you up on this beautiful day, 'The only way is up' by Yazz and the Plastic Population." The familiar music filtered through the tinny radio alarm clock.

The shiver from his dream and the sudden piercing of the radio alarm coincided to jolt Matt from his sleep. As he slowly opened his eyes, he had the strange sensation of trying to recapture the dream whilst it simultaneously drifted from his mind until the image was nothing but a vague memory.

Matt lay in bed staring at the ceiling, and let the lyrics of the song drift over him as he contemplated getting up.

Another day at work. He closed his eyes for one last time, before he opened them again, sighed, threw back the covers, and swung his legs over the edge of the bed.

He took a good look at himself in the mirror as he washed and shaved, before hitting the shower. As the water ran over his body, a flicker of his dream returned to him. He remembered being in an elevator as it crashed through the roof of a tall building. He shook his head at the absurdity of the notion that he could dream of such a thing, smiling as it reminded him of his favorite book from his childhood. He had read and reread *Charlie and the Chocolate Factory* so many times when he was young that he could quote huge chunks of it, much like older people quote Shakespeare. It was a nice memory. He smiled to himself as he rubbed the foam from his head and it splashed noisily onto the floor of the shower tray.

The day was much like any other. After the habitual morning greetings, comparing notes about last night's TV, and the gossip from the leaving drinks of someone or other, Matt and his colleagues in the office got into the rhythm of the day.

The calls from customers came and went mostly without incident, the team putting the sales training they had just learnt into practice in an attempt to achieve their team target for the month. They were in week two, and so far so good. They were on target, and just behind Tim's team who were in first place on the sales leader board. There was a genuine enthusiasm in Matt's team that with a little extra effort, a little extra time on the phone for everyone, and a small prayer that someone on Tim's team might catch the bug that was going around the office, Matt's team could actually win the incentive spa weekend that was on offer. With a team of six people, five of whom were women, this was a sales incentive that (unlike most of the others), was genuinely worth winning. The team were in a positive, go-getting mood.

Matt, on the other hand, was not. Whilst his team were answering the constantly ringing phones, he had been called into a room by his boss, Jo.

After the obligatory small talk, Jo said that she had some feedback for him.

"OK," said Matt, unconsciously bracing himself. He had no idea what was coming.

"You know that we were looking to promote someone into the available Sales Manager role?" said Jo, raising her voice at the end of the sentence to half suggest that she was asking a question. Matt nodded, smiling expectantly.

"Well, I want to let you know that the promotion panel have decided to give the promotion to Tim."

Matt took a breath but, before he could respond, she continued.

"I'm sorry, I know you really wanted it."

Matt looked to the ceiling, and tried to remain composed. Jo sat in silence and looked at him, waiting for him to speak.

"I don't believe this," said Matt finally. "Am I ever going to get promoted? I mean, what's Tim got that I haven't? Why not me?" The disappointment was clear in Matt's tone, and he was finding it difficult not to get angry. Although she had anticipated this reaction, Jo knew that she needed to tread carefully: he was genuinely upset.

"It's not a competition," she said softly in an attempt to comfort him.

"We had to select the person that we thought would do the best job, Matt, and the panel just didn't think you were ready yet," she continued.

"What do you mean—not ready? I've been here longer than Tim!" he exclaimed, raising his voice a little.

"I know," Jo replied, "It's not about length of service, and it's not just about figures and hitting the targets either, although obviously that's important."

Jo had captured Matt's attention. How could promotion not be about achieving targets?

"It's more about the other things, the little things," she said.

Matt shook his head. "I'm sorry, I don't understand," he said, looking to Jo for an answer.

She shuffled in her chair a little uncomfortably. She took a deep breath as if to collect her thoughts.

"OK," she said, "here's the deal." Matt had never seen Jo look flustered like this before. She looked like she was going to tell him something significant.

"Tim's a very outgoing person, he gets involved in things, people know who he is and what he's doing. Some of the people on the promotion panel don't even know who you are, Matt, and when there's only one spot available, and everyone around the table knows Tim and has a good view of him, well, there's no competition."

Matt sat back in his chair. He appreciated Jo's directness. This was a good argument, and he knew that it was true. Matt focused on hitting his targets every month, whilst Tim spent time chatting to each of the Sales Managers at their desks, moving from one to the next through the day, like a bee buzzing from flower to flower searching for pollen.

"I'm sorry to be the bringer of bad news, Matt, but do you understand what I mean?" asked Jo.

"I think so," said Matt tentatively. In truth, he wasn't really sure whether he did or not. He was still blindsided by the news that someone whom he had helped to train when he joined just under two years ago had been promoted ahead of him.

Jo smiled. "Thanks Matt. Oh—and well done on your figures by the way—looks like your girls are really focused on that trip to the spa." Jo smiled and touched Matt affectionately on the shoulder as she left the room.

Matt stared at the fading Monet print on the wall in front of him, and collected his thoughts.

Matt left the room and went straight outside and into the Starbucks that was situated conveniently across the road. With it being so close to the office, Matt was a regular here, to the extent that the staff not only knew him by name, they also knew his choice of coffee—which made him feel comfortable. He certainly wouldn't dream of going anywhere else for his coffee, even though there were other choices just moments away. This was *his* place.

He stood in the small queue and waited to be served. Ben, the Barista, greeted Matt with a warm smile. "Hey Matt, how you doing—the usual?" he shouted. Matt nodded and gave Ben a thumbs-up. The mammoth stainless-steel coffee machine roared into action.

Matt stood and waited, alone with his thoughts.

The voice seemed to come out of nowhere. "You look like you've got the weight of the world on your shoulders."

Matt turned his head round and saw an older gentleman standing a few feet behind him in the line. The man made quite an impression: late fifties, pure white hair, and a neatly kept, powder-white goatee beard. The man had a charming, eccentric air: sharp navy suit, and eye-catching, unusual shoes. He cut quite a dashing figure. Though there was something familiar about him.

Matt smiled. "One of those days," he said, shrugging his shoulders, and turned back to face Ben as he worked away with the foaming milk.

"Oh, we all have those now and again," said the older man.

"I guess," said Matt, with a polite smile, half turning his head back toward the older man.

The two men stood in silence next to each other, watching the barista in action.

"Do you know what latte means in French?" Matt turned and faced the man.

"You paid too much for that coffee," said the older man smirking.

The two men looked at each other and laughed, breaking the ice between them.

"Edward Evans," said the older man offering Matt his hand. "Matt Eliott."

Ben snapped lids onto the two men's coffees, and placed them on the brightly colored ledge next to the coffee machine. "Have a good day. See you Matt," said Ben. Matt winked back at him. "Cheers Ben."

Edward gestured towards Ben. "Looks like you're a regular here then?" he laughed.

Matt smiled. "Yeah, I've been coming here for ages—I like it here."

"Good to have somewhere you can retreat to when it gets too much in there." Edward gestured toward the tall glass building next door, Matt's office.

"Absolutely!" said Matt smiling, sensing that Edward did just the same.

"You looked like you had a lot on your mind over there,"

said Edward nodding his head in the direction of the waiting customers.

Matt knew that Edward was right, but wasn't sure whether he wanted to get into this conversation with someone he had met just a few minutes before. He had to get back to the office: the early lunch relief on the desk would be happening soon.

He made a snap decision to respond to the old man's assertion.

"Bit of a long story, but I've just been told by my boss that I wasn't going to get the promotion that I was hoping for." He shrugged his shoulders.

"I see," said Edward, hoping the silence would encourage Matt to continue with his story. Matt checked his watch, then, deciding he could delay going back to the office for a little longer, moved over to the velvet chairs that were just next to them. He sat down and Edward did the same.

"Well, I joined the company about a year before this guy, Tim, and my boss has just told me that they have decided to give the one open Sales Manager position to him. I just don't understand it, I'm as good as he is, in fact I'm better than Tim in lots of ways. I even trained him when he started."

"You sound really annoyed about it," said Edward.

"I am!" he exclaimed. "I'm getting the results, and I know I can do it—I just don't know why it's not happening for me."

The two men sat in silence for a second.

"You make it sound like it's something that you have no control over."

"What do you mean?" enquired Matt, with a slightly accusatory tone. He didn't expect to be challenged by someone he had just met in the coffee shop.

"You said it's not happening for *me*—as if it's something that's out of your control."

"Well it is—*I* don't decide whether I get promoted, do I? I really want to—but it's up to this panel of managers to approve me."

"That's true, but you *can* influence their decision." At that moment Edward captured Matt's full attention.

"What do you mean?" said Matt, sounding a little confused.

Edward sidelined the young man's question.

"Tell me more about this Tim chap that you mentioned a minute ago," invited Edward.

Matt stopped for a moment, and looked like he was picturing Tim in his mind. "Um, I'm not sure really. I mean he does the same kind of work that I do, he joined the company a year or so after I did. He's a nice guy, we get on well."

"What else?" invited Edward.

Matt continued, "Well he always seems to be talking to one of the Sales Managers by the coffee machine or in the corridor, and he does this other thing—he sends Jo an email every week—'Tim's ticker-tape' he calls it." Matt smiled wryly and shook his head with a mixture of sarcasm and disbelief.

"What's that?" questioned Edward.

"Oh, some stupid little gimmick he came up with—a kind of update that he puts together for her: sales figures, people issues, little projects that he's involved in, that sort of thing." Matt sounded dismissive.

Edward noted Matt's slightly sarcastic tone and challenged further. "How do you know he does that?"

"Oh, Jo mentions it from time to time in meetings."

Edward moved on.

"OK, what else does Tim do that makes him different to you?"

The younger man thought for a moment before answering. "He certainly spends more time with Jo than I do. I mean we all have our 'one to one' meeting with her for an hour every week, but he often pops over to her desk in between those ..." Edward stopped Matt again. "How long does he spend with her when he does that? You know, on average?" asked the older man.

"Not long," said Matt, "I would say five minutes, maybe a touch more."

"OK, and do you know what they talk about?"

"I've overheard the conversation occasionally, and often it's about nothing, you know—could be chat about the TV they've watched, or Tim asking about something that he knew Jo was doing that weekend. Sometimes it's work related though—I overheard them discussing a difficult phone call that Tim had with a client just yesterday, in fact."

"Sounds like this Tim has consciously worked hard to build up a good relationship with Jo," said Edward. He was determined for the young man to view the situation from a slightly different perspective.

"I guess so," said Matt dismissively, "but I'm not there to 'build good relationships' with my boss, I'm there to work. To achieve my targets."

Edward smiled and looked Matt straight in the eye. "And Tim started after you and got promoted before you, you say? Mmmm ..." Edward's voice had a sarcastic tone to it as he stroked his goatee. The moment was not lost on Matt.

"What? You think his getting close to Jo has helped him get promoted?"

"Well," said Edward, "let's think about it another way." He paused and for a short moment there was silence between the two men as Matt looked at Edward and waited with anticipation.

"Let's say you owned your own company and you had

built a successful business. The business grew and you knew that you couldn't continue to do everything yourself, so you would need to hand over some responsibility to someone else in order for you to focus on more pressing issues at hand."

"Right," said Matt, who had clearly been drawn into the story. He leaned toward Edward as he continued.

"You have a couple of people that you could potentially hand over to."

"OK."

"The first person was someone who was the most knowledgeable about the company, had been there quite some time, and was good at their job, solid, a safe pair of hands. They would always deliver on time, attend meetings and contribute, and did exactly what was expected of them."

"Sounds good," said Matt.

Edward nodded in agreement, and continued his story.

"The other candidate also was good at their job, achieved all their targets, attended the meetings that they should and contributed well, just like the other person. But this person also spent time in getting to know people outside of their immediate circle of colleagues, made it their business to know which elements of their work were of particular interest to you, his or her boss, and made sure that they gave you regular updates on how they were doing. Nothing formal or dramatic—just by sending a short email or dropping by your desk, that sort of thing."

"Now, tell me," continued Edward, "as the owner of the company, and this person's boss, how would you feel about them?"

Matt paused for a moment before replying: "Well I guess I would think that the second person had made more of an effort, would be more connected to what was going on than the first person you mentioned—and that they took more of an interest in things that were outside their job."

"OK, good. What else? How would their working this way actually make you *feel* about them?" encouraged Edward.

"Well I'd feel supported, I'd feel comfortable, I guess I'd feel as though I could really rely on them—that they 'got it'."

Edward stood in front of Matt in silence, giving him a moment to process his answer.

After a few moments, Matt emerged from his moment of self-reflection.

"I get it. Tim's like the second person in your example: he did more than 'the job'—he supported Jo, his boss, so that she knew what was going on, making sure that she looked good in front of her boss. He spent time getting to know other people in the company, so when it came to promotion time, people knew who he was and could give their support to his promotion. They're not going to support my promotion, because they don't know who I am!"

Edward laughed, "Exactly!" He nodded and smiled at Matt in the way a proud parent would. He was pleased to see the, albeit small, change in Matt from when they had first met, when he seemed so despondent. He was glad that the young man had finally understood that his not getting promoted was not personal, that there was a reason for it.

"Tim didn't work any *harder* than me, he just focused on things other than the 'work'."

"Right," said Edward warmly, touching Matt on the arm. "Most people are competent at their job—in fact the quality of their work is rarely the differentiating factor."

"So what is?" enquired Matt, turning to look directly at Edward.

"Well it's rarely one thing," said Edward. "In fact, it's a number of things, each of them very important and powerful in their own right."

"So what are they?" said Matt, laughing. He hit the arm of the velvet chair with the palm of his hand a few times in mock anger. "C'mon, I want to get promoted!"

Edward laughed.

"OK," relented Edward. "It's a secret, but a secret that everyone knows."

Matt was confused. "What do you mean?"

Edward continued: "Everyone knows what to do. They just don't realize they do, because they rarely stop to think about it." Edward could see that Matt was intrigued.

"I'm all ears," said the young man.

Edward smiled. "So you want to know the secret of how some people make it and others don't?"

"Yes please."

"You want to know how some people keep moving up the corporate ladder while others stall halfway?" he teased.

Matt's eyes widened as he nodded.

"The secret of how some people, who may be no better on the job than you are, appear to float past you on their way to the top."

"Yes, yes, yes!" shouted Matt, laughing.

Edward smiled and beckoned Matt closer. "Well, my friend," he said as he looked deep into Matt's eyes, "let me tell you the secret of career helium."

Quality of work
is rarely the
differentiating
factor.

M att was gripped.

"Career *what?*" he questioned. Matt felt like he'd misunderstood the punch line of a joke.

Edward repeated himself. "Career *helium,*" he said, his tone of voice placing an obvious emphasis on the word helium.

"How many jobs have you had?" the older man asked Matt.

"This is my third," he answered quickly, keen to get through Edward's line of questioning so he could hear more about this strange helium notion.

"And whilst you were working hard in each of these jobs, I'm going to guess that you have watched as other people have risen further, and quicker, through the organization than you have. They seem to get on quicker than you, yet the difference in their performance on the job is negligible. Would that be right?"

"Oh yes—definitely," replied Matt, a little taken aback that Edward's synopsis was quite so akin with Matt's own experience.

"Well, career helium changes the way you view work. Once people discover the secret, they never work in the same

way again. You see, getting ahead isn't just about performance or hitting targets."

Matt couldn't help himself interrupting Edward: "What do
you mean? If I don't perform, I'm out! I see someone leave every
week because they haven't hit their targets!" he exclaimed.

"I dare say you do," continued Edward, "and indeed that's
the way it should be. If you want to tick along, get paid every
month, then that is indeed what you need to do—focus on
your targets, and the salary will come. But if that is your sole
focus, then it will take you a lot longer to work your way up
the corporate ladder. Career helium is the secret formula for
accelerating your success. Provided that you are performing,
and achieving what's expected of you, then you can adopt
the secret of career helium immediately, and you will soon
reap the benefits."

"So, what is it?" Matt wanted an answer. He wanted something tangible.

"Well," replied Edward, sensing Matt's impatience, "It's a
combination of factors, all of which are important individu-
ally, and even more powerful when combined. A secret recipe,
if you will." Edward paused. He picked up the burgundy
journal that he had laid on the coffee table in front of them
when they first sat down together. Their coffee mugs had long
since been cleared away.

Edward turned to a fresh page, reached inside his suit
jacket pocket and pulled out a Montblanc pen. Matt looked at
the sleek black pen in admiration—he had promised himself
one whenever he got promoted—he thought they looked so
elegant and professional. Tim already had one.

Edward's pen hovered over the page. He looked at the young
man.

Getting ahead isn't just about performance or hitting targets.

"Career helium is made up of five very simple elements." Edward's speech slowed as he slipped unconsciously into coach and mentor mode. Matt, without thinking, responded and moved closer to the page, supporting his head with the palm of his hand. He focused his attention completely on Edward, eagerly awaiting these secrets.

The two men sat in silence. Matt watched carefully as the older man began to draw a diagram on the page in front of him. As the image grew, Matt thought he recognized it from his school days. He waited to speak until Edward had finished.

"That looks like something from one of my old chemistry lessons," Matt said warily as the memories of struggling at school with one of his least favorite subjects flooded back to him.

Edward smiled. "Similar," he said. "Allow me to explain." Matt wished he hadn't jumped in. He forced himself to sit and listen—he didn't want to miss a thing.

Edward had sketched a diagram on the page: a central ball, with five hoops circling it, with a smaller ball on each hoop. The diagram looked like it should be animated, with the smaller balls in the hoops spinning around the larger one. On each of the smaller balls, Edward had written single letters, shorthand for the words that he had written alongside.

"Let me talk you through it," said Edward, breaking Matt's eye contact from the page.

"*This* is the composition of career helium," he explained.

"At the core of career helium is AR^2. If you adopt the notion of career helium successfully, then this is what you will reap—Achievement, Recognition, and Reward." Edward looked at Matt for some confirmation that he was following his explanation. He received the reply that he was looking for.

"OK" said Matt, nodding.

Edward continued. He pointed to each of the smaller balls in turn, using his pen as a pointer: "*Expectations, Profile, Politics, Networking, and Boss.*" Finally he pointed to all the lines connecting AR² with each of the solid balls. "And each of these hoops represents context."

He had Matt's full attention.

"Let me explain how they all fit together," continued Edward.

"Those that progress through an organization do so because they know that performance on the job is not a differentiator. What differentiates one person from another—is their ability to integrate the five elements of career helium into the way they work. You'll notice that your performance

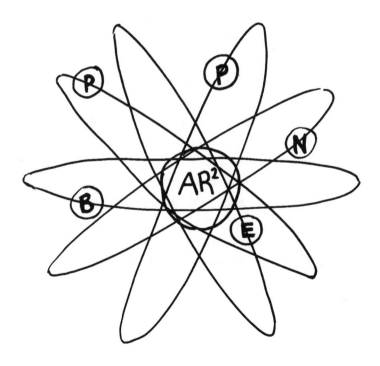

on the job, as such, is not mentioned in career helium—that's because it's taken as a given that you perform. You need to be performing what's expected of you for career helium to be effective for you. What will accelerate your career is your ability to ..." Edward paused, and pointed his pen to the *Expectations* ball, "... understand the expectations that people have of you. Achieve, or even better, *exceed* those expectations." He pointed to the other balls in turn with his pen.

"Understand your boss and what *they* need to achieve, and then help them to achieve their own goals," he said, pointing to the ball marked *Boss*.

He moved his pen to the next ball, marked with a P for *Profile*. "Ensure that you know who the key people are that can positively influence your career, and that they know what you are doing."

Edward continued, his pen drifting over to the penultimate ball, marked with an N. "... that you are able to support the development of your profile within the organization by *Networking* with those who can help you to succeed. And," he continued, "that you are conscious of the *Politics* that goes on around you all the time, so you are able to manage it in a positive way that moves you closer to your own goals." His pen rested on the final ball.

"The important thing is that all this needs to happen in a way that suits your organization—the context that I mentioned—so knowing how it 'ticks,' and working within those 'parameters of acceptability,' is key."

He turned his attention away from the page, and back to Matt.

"You see, my friend, there's a big difference between what gets you *paid*, and what gets you *ahead*. Most people focus on what gets them *paid*—just 'doing the job.'

"What gets you ahead is career helium: the five elements that, if you pay attention to them, and manage them, will accelerate your growth and development through your organization. This," paused Edward, "is the difference that makes the difference."

There's a big difference between what gets you _paid_ and what gets you _ahead_.

Matt sank into the purple velvet chair. He needed a moment to process everything that he had just heard. Edward sat patiently opposite him. He was very aware that this was a lot to take in.

It all made sense to Matt, but he had so many things buzzing around in his mind at once, he found it difficult to focus his thoughts. Whilst listening to Edward talking through the career helium diagram, Matt kept thinking about Tim. Tim had helped Jo to achieve her objectives; he networked with all the Sales Managers; and it was certainly evident that he had built himself a profile because everyone on the promotion panel knew who he was. It was beginning to make sense. He could see that Tim had already put these ideas into practice, whether consciously or unconsciously, and had certainly begun to reap the benefits.

Matt felt frustrated with himself that he had got it so wrong. All this time, in this job and the others before it, he had focused on achieving his immediate results, believing that if he "did a good job" he would automatically get on—more responsibility, promotion and, with that, a higher salary. Everything that his new friend had explained to him made sense. However, it now seemed that this was the starting

Achieving what you
are employed to do
is just the beginning.

point, rather than the end point: achieving what you are employed to do is just the beginning.

As Matt looked at Edward, he had a flicker of déjà vu. He felt that he had seen him before, but couldn't place him somehow. He was normally so good with recalling names and faces.

Matt pulled himself up from the enveloping comfort of the velvet chair, and closer to the table where the career helium sketch was still sitting in front of Edward.

"What do you think?" asked Edward softly.

"It makes perfect sense," replied Matt. "But it's weird—it feels like everything that I've done all these years has been wrong."

Edward smiled. "It's not that it's wrong, Matt, it's just a different way of looking at things. Everyone is programmed from when they are young to 'work hard at school,' and people rationalize that as getting good exam results; and then when they reach work, that becomes translated as achieving your objectives, hitting your sales targets, reducing your patients' waiting times, or whatever's relevant for your job."

Matt smiled in recognition—he could see his parents in his mind's eye telling him to "work hard at school" when he was younger—as if that was the sole route to success.

"No one ever gets to learn about career helium until it's too late, and even if they do, they keep the secret for themselves and don't share it with many other people, to minimize the 'competition,'" said Edward.

This was beginning to make sense for Matt. He smiled.

"So how do I make it happen for me?" he asked.

"I'd be delighted to be your guide," offered Edward.

"I'd be honored," replied Matt, smiling.

The two men shook hands warmly and made for the door.

Quite out of the blue, Matt remembered one of his mother's favorite sayings: *today is the first day of the rest of your life.* At that moment, this familiar saying took on a whole new meaning for Matt.

He smiled as he walked outside into the sunshine with his new mentor.

The two men reached the big glass door of the office. They hadn't spoken much since leaving the coffee shop a few minutes ago. The silence between them was a comfortable one though, for Edward knew that Matt was still processing what he had shared with him.

Edward broke the silence. "I'll give you some time to let our discussion sink in, then we can get started."

"That would be great—although I do want to get started as soon as possible," said Matt enthusiastically.

"OK, well how about we meet tomorrow at around 11 AM?" Edward gestured his head toward the Starbucks across the road. "Bring an open mind." Edward paused. Matt braced himself for another pearl of wisdom from his new friend. "And an open wallet—the lattes are on you!" They both laughed, and said their goodbyes.

Matt got back to the office to find everyone crowded around Tim's desk. He was accepting handshakes and kisses from his colleagues. His promotion to Sales Manager had just been announced.

As the crowd began to disperse, Matt approached Tim with an extended hand. Tim looked cautious—he was surprised that Matt appeared to be taking his promotion in such a positive way. He had noticed that Matt hadn't been at his desk for the last half hour or so, and had assumed that he had gone to lick his wounds. Tim had anticipated that Matt may become a little frosty, and that perhaps their friendship would change. After all, if it wasn't for Matt training Tim so well when he joined, he probably wouldn't have been promoted so quickly. He did feel a tinge of guilt.

Tim smiled, a touch of relief showing in his face, and accepted Matt's hand—shaking it warmly.

"Well done Tim—really pleased for you," said Matt. He smiled, summoning all the sincerity he could.

"Thanks—I really appreciate that," Tim replied, with a distinct emphasis that he hoped Matt would pick up. As the two men greeted each other, the crowd around Tim's desk was dissipating—everyone in the office knew that this was a potentially sensitive conversation, and respectfully gave them some space. Everyone's focus was firmly on Matt.

"I couldn't have done it without your help," Tim added.

"Thanks for that—but I just got you started. In fact—you've taught me a few things too," Matt smiled, and Tim looked confused.

"Really?"

"Oh sure."

Tim expected Matt to continue, but after a short silence that felt a whole lot longer than it actually was, it was clear that he wasn't going to add anything else to this ambiguous statement. Matt wanted to leave a little mystery in the air. He wanted Tim to think that maybe there was more to Matt than met the eye.

Right now, after his meeting with Edward, he truly believed there was.

The next day, Matt woke with a positivity that he hadn't experienced for a long time. Even the crowded conditions of his morning journey on the train couldn't dent his enthusiasm. He wished the minutes away until he could take a break to go and meet Edward across the road. The morning seemed to crawl—like the last few days before Christmas when you are six years old.

Soon, it was five to 11, and Matt collected his notepad and his pen, and made his way out of the building. He got to Starbucks dead on time, but after searching both upstairs and downstairs, Edward was nowhere to be found. Matt could feel his heart beating faster in his chest—where was he? Surely he couldn't have forgotten?

Matt decided to wait, and joined the line. Just as he was giving his order to the pretty Italian girl behind the counter, he heard a voice behind him.

"I'll have a skinny vanilla latte—and this young man's paying."

Matt turned to find Edward standing behind him, smiling.

"How the devil are you this fine morning?" the older man asked.

"Great now you're here," said Matt, relieved. "I got here at

11, and when you weren't here, I thought you'd maybe forgotten about me."

"Oh, I would never do that," said Edward. "The first rule of success is to always do what you say you are going to do. If you can't do that, you might as well just pack up and go home!"

Matt smiled in agreement. He knew that Edward was right—his father had drilled that thought into him when he was younger, along with his other favorite saying: "If a job's worth doing, it's worth doing well." Simple as they were, these nuggets had served Matt well.

The two men took their coffees and found a couple of comfy-looking velvet chairs tucked away in the corner.

"Perfect," said Edward.

They made themselves comfortable, and Matt sat expectantly in front of his mentor.

Edward got straight down to business. "Before we start, there's something I need to make sure you understand."

This sounded serious, Matt thought. He put down the wooden stirrer, and fixed his attention on Edward. "OK."

"You need to understand that career helium is not a quick fix." Edward paused to make sure that his point had sunk in, then he continued, "Success is rarely something that comes overnight. Success rewards those who invest, and wait."

Matt looked a little puzzled.

"The things that I'm going to share with you are not quick fixes: you will need to understand them, and look for opportunities to apply them. Sometimes, you will need to invest time in order to reap your reward. Career helium is like a good red wine in that sense. You can drink a red wine fairly immediately, or if you allow time for it to ferment and mature, the result will be so much more satisfying. Career

Success is rarely something that comes overnight. Success rewards those who invest, and wait.

helium is just like that. The foundation of career helium is relationships—and relationships take some time to mature— just like that red wine." Edward stopped for a moment. He wanted to make sure Matt understood this—it was crucial to his being able to use career helium successfully.

"OK, I understand—relationships aren't just formed overnight—it takes time to get to know someone."

"Right—and that's why reaping the benefits of career helium requires a little investment up front."

"OK, I get it," said the young man, "so what you're saying is that I shouldn't expect things to happen immediately?"

Edward bowed his head slowly in agreement. "Exactly. Now you are ready to learn."

Matt shifted his weight in the chair, with an enthusiastic little bounce. He wanted the lesson to begin.

Edward reached into his slim portfolio and took out the thick, expensive-looking journal that he had sketched in the last time the two had met. Matt noticed the gold embossed lettering on the back of the journal—"Smythson of Bond Street." The journal looked luxurious, and matched Edward's air of professional elegance perfectly. The luxurious burgundy journal joined the Montblanc pen on Matt's "must have" list.

Edward found the page where he had drawn the career helium diagram the day before.

"You remember the premise of career helium—that these five elements are the elements that will fuel your rise through the organization? If you pay attention to these things, and put into practice the simple strategies I'm about to share with you, you will achieve greater, and more sustained, success than others."

"I certainly do remember," laughed Matt. "In fact, I've thought of nothing else since we met yesterday."

Edward smiled: "I know just what you mean. When I discovered the secret of career helium for the first time, that's exactly what happened for me. It was as if someone had flicked a switch and illuminated the world with a brightness and intensity that I had never experienced before. I noticed things that were always there—but that I had never seen before. It quite changed my life."

Matt sat entranced.

"I changed my approach, I changed my understanding of what was important in getting ahead. All of this," Edward gently gestured toward his exquisitely tailored clothes and his Smythson journal, "I owe to the secret of career helium."

Edward appeared to reflect on that past for a moment before continuing. "Of course, you must remember that the basics have to be in place first—you need to be performing in your job first for career helium to work for you."

"I remember you mentioned that yesterday—that's not a problem for me," said Matt.

"Excellent. Then I think you're ready to get started!" Edward's tone was brimming with enthusiasm.

He pointed to one of the five "balls" on the career helium diagram. "Let me take you through these elements one by one. Let's focus on the first element: *Expectation*." Edward drew a circle around the word, laid his pen on the page, and fixed his gaze firmly on Matt.

"What does *expectation* mean to you?" Edward sat back slowly in his chair—clearly shifting the focus in the conversation from himself to Matt. He waited while Matt considered the question for a moment. The young man took more than a moment to answer.

"Mmmm. I think expectation is a belief that someone has that you are going to be doing something for them, or perhaps they are going to be receiving something from you?" Matt was hesitant in his answer. He wasn't sure whether this was what Edward was expecting—he had never been asked this kind of question before.

"Good. Do you know what, specifically, others are expecting of you?"

Matt was even more flummoxed. "Er, I don't know—sometimes they tell you and sometimes they don't."

"Good. If someone tells you what they expect of you, then you can achieve it, right?"

"Sure," Matt replied.

"And if they have expectations of you and don't share them, how easy is it to deliver for them then?"

"Well, it's difficult, if not impossible. I mean—how can you achieve something if you don't know what it is?"

"Exactly—that's the most important thing about expectations. If you know what's expected of you, you can deliver it. If you don't know what that is, it makes it very difficult! But, often, people at work—your boss or colleagues, for example—will have expectations of you and your performance, but they will keep them to themselves. They will judge you against these *invisible* expectations, but will rarely share this benchmark with you ..."

"That doesn't sound very fair to me," interrupted Matt.

"No, it doesn't does it?" replied Edward. "Let me take you back to our conversation yesterday. You said that the promotion panel had promoted Tim because of the approach that he took over and above his job, yes?"

"Yeah, that's right."

"Well—sounds like they had a pretty clear expectation in their mind of what it took to get promoted, doesn't it?"

The penny dropped for Matt. "Yes! They probably didn't share this with Tim but from what Jo said to me, the panel had a pretty clear idea of what they were looking for in their successful candidate."

"Now, Tim probably didn't know what these expectations

were, but he did a good second guess of what they might be. And sounds like he got it right—he got promoted. Conversely, you didn't stack up against that expectation, so you didn't get promoted."

"I see." Matt sank thoughtfully into his chair.

"Does that sound fair to you?" asked Edward.

"No, it doesn't. It sounds cruel, actually. How can you have a guideline in your mind of what you expect someone to do, and then not share that with them—how can you hit a target if you can't see it?" Edward could sense that Matt was getting a little frustrated at the apparent unjustness of the situation.

"It is just like that—it's asking someone to hit a target, and then blindfolding them!" Edward chuckled, and infected Matt with his laughter, which lightened the mood between them.

"Knowing what the expectations are of you is the foundation of career helium—you need to remove the blindfold that others place on you, so that you know exactly what to deliver."

Matt was feverishly making notes as Edward was speaking—everything that he had said so far made perfect sense to Matt.

"So, how do you remove the blindfold?" asked Edward, interrupting Matt's scribbling on his notepad.

"Well, it's unlikely that these expectations are written down anywhere, so I guess the only way that you will learn what expectations someone has of you is to ask them."

Edward nodded in agreement. "Except," he added, "in the case of *universal expectations*."

"What are they?" asked Matt.

"Have you seen those 'Our Behaviors' posters around the building?" asked Edward.

"Sure—haven't really taken that much notice to be honest." Matt shrugged.

Expectations: remove the blindfold that others place on you, so you know exactly what the benchmark is.

"Oh really?" said Edward, sounding a little surprised. "That's a shame—because that's your first set of expectations right there: the universal expectations."

"Isn't that just corporate claptrap?" Matt smiled, but Edward clearly wasn't amused.

"That's what most people think—we all walk past these posters a hundred times a day. We see them so often they become invisible to us. Do you know what these behaviors are?" he asked, challenging his young friend.

Matt thought for a second. "Er, teamwork, um, isn't there something in there about respect ..." His voice trailed off. He was embarrassed that he couldn't recall the information that he was exposed to a couple of hundred times a week. He could see that Edward was disappointed in him.

Edward looked straight at Matt and recited the behaviors. "Teamwork, respect for each other, working with integrity, being courageous, taking accountability, doing the right thing, and putting the client first. To be precise," recounted Edward.

Matt was embarrassed.

"I bet that your friend Tim took time to read them," added the older man sarcastically.

"OK, OK, I get it, but why are they so important?" Matt asked.

"Well, those posters represent the organization saying to you: 'This is how we want you to go about doing business on our behalf—this is what we expect of you.' These are the universal expectations, Matt—the expectations that the organization has of everyone who works there—it's universal for all. It's laid out for you in black and white on almost every wall in the building. And you've been ignoring it!" Matt looked at the floor.

"I bet that this is part of the expectations that the promotion panel were using when they compared you and Tim. And from what you've told me earlier—it looks like Tim has read those posters, and has integrated the spirit of what those behaviors are about into his approach to work."

Matt had begun to realize that he had a lot to learn. Edward was right—those posters were highlighting very clear expectations. Matt had received a copy when they were introduced about a year ago, but he had thrown it in the trash, more or less straightaway. And he knew a lot of other people that had done the same. It was slowly dawning on him that he had thrown away a big heads-up from the organization in terms of the expectations that it had of him. He was frustrated with himself.

"A few minutes ago, you said that the universal expectations were the first set of expectations—are there more then?" he asked.

"Yes. Of course there are many different sets of expectations that are placed on you—every member of your team would have expectations of you, for example, but there are three important sets of expectations that provide the helium to float your career: the universal expectations, the role expectations, and the niche expectations."

Matt made a note of this distinction in his notebook. "The niche expectations?" he queried.

"We'll get to that—one at a time."

"OK, well I can see the universal expectations are pretty straightforward ..."

Edward interrupted him. "When you actually take notice of what's under your nose," he teased.

"Quite," continued Matt, smiling, "but the role expectations? Are they the expectations placed on you by others for the role, the job, that you are doing?"

"Exactly. What do you think those expectations could be?" asked Edward.

"OK, I think that's an easy one." Matt was relieved to have a question from his mentor that he could answer without worrying whether he would be way off track. "I get set targets for the year—and then for every month—so these would be the role expectations, right?"

"Yes, exactly. Knowing what you need to deliver." Edward nodded.

"If you know what your sales targets are, and you know what the universal expectations are—what else could there be?" asked Matt.

Edward smiled. "Now, this is the clever bit. The devil is always in the detail, my friend. Your boss is Jo, right?"

"Uh-huh."

"OK, don't you think that Jo will also have some expectations of her own—you know, the way she likes things done in her team, her own little pet standards—things that are important to just her?"

"I see what you mean. Well, there are a few things—she's a stickler for time keeping—she hates it if you are late for one of her team meetings, for example."

"Right—well this is an example of what I call the niche expectations. Those little things—the expectations that someone will have of you that are specific just to them."

Edward began to draw a kind of cone shape in his journal, and divided it into three sections—one broad at the top of the cone, one in the middle, and one towards the bottom, where the cone narrowed to a tip. Matt copied it into his own notebook, watching as the diagram emerged on Edward's page.

"So, in a nutshell, there will be the *universal* expectations." He added each to his diagram as he spoke. "The *role* expectations—

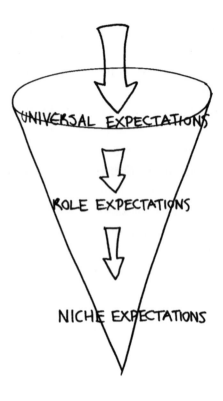

those expectations that are placed on you in the role you perform, and then the *niche* expectations—those little standards that form your Boss's personal management style." Matt was nodding—he could think back to a few examples that supported what Edward was explaining. It made sense to him.

Matt let out a sigh and flopped back in his chair. "Phew!"

Edward smiled. He knew that this was a lot to take in, so he gave his young friend a moment to absorb everything that he had taught him. He took the opportunity to drain the remainder of his coffee cup.

"So, what's your next step?" Edward kick-started the conversation.

"Well, I know what the universal expectations are now, I know my role expectations, but I don't know anything about the niche expectations that Jo has of me." Matt was pleased with his summary.

"So how are you going to get some clarity on Jo's niche expectations?"

"Well, I think the only way that I can do that is to ask her."

"Absolutely," Edward smiled. He took great joy in watching his protégé's journey of discovery and development. "While you're there, I would also clarify the role expectations with her—just to be sure." Edward tapped the diagram in front of him. "If you are going to be having a conversation with her about expectations—this would be a good opportunity to make sure that there is nothing else further up the cone that you are unaware of. Leave no stone unturned."

Matt nodded and added to the notes on his pad.

"Do you think that Jo will be expecting you to have this conversation with her?" Edward asked.

"Not sure. Probably not."

"I would guess not. If you haven't spoken with her about this kind of thing before, then you may well surprise her with your level of focus—particularly when it comes to asking her to share her niche expectations with you," commented Edward.

"Mmmm, you're probably right."

"So you'll need to give her some context. Explain that you are focused on addressing the feedback that she gave you after the promotion panel, and that you want to be clear what expectations she has of you and every aspect of your performance," offered the older man.

"OK, this is good, really useful, thanks." Matt finished his notes, closed his notepad, and gave Edward a smile that had a hint of mental exhaustion about it.

"My pleasure—I look forward to hearing how the conversation goes."

The two men agreed to meet again, once Matt had had his "expectations" conversation with Jo.

J ust as Edward had predicted, Jo was indeed surprised by Matt's question.

"What's brought this on, Matt? You've never asked me anything like this before?"

"Well, let's just say that I'm looking at things in a slightly different way from now on—you know, since our conversation about me, and Tim, and everything." His voice faded away slightly at the end of the sentence—a detail that didn't escape Jo.

"I understand," she said sympathetically.

And she did. Jo had watched others rise past her for a number of years, and never knew what she could do to replicate their success. She tried working longer hours, but that hadn't worked. She tried smashing her targets, but that had taken her only so far. She had been at a complete loss as to what she could do to move her career forward when she met a man who had shared with her a secret, a secret that she had held dear ever since. He showed her a different approach, one that had enabled her to reap the success that she was searching for. She had achieved the accolade of being the youngest woman ever within the company to be promoted to Sector Sales Manager as a result, and had leapfrogged some of her colleagues in the promotion stakes. She thought of her mentor often, and the powerful secrets that he had shared with her. Since then, she had floated steadily up the corporate ladder, just as Edward Evans said she would.

Jo and Matt sat together for some time as she clarified her expectations of his role, and shared with him the expectations that she personally valued from one of her team. Matt found the conversation very useful, and was surprised at how comfortable Jo was in sharing her niche expectations with him. Clearly this was something that she had given careful thought to previously. There were some things that were important to her that he wasn't aware of, and hadn't considered before. He added the feedback that Jo gave him to the notes that he had taken during his conversation with Edward a few days previously. He was certainly going to change the way that he worked with her.

Jo was pleased that Matt was taking such a proactive approach to developing his career—she had always had a soft spot for him. He was sincere, and focused on realizing his potential, and she liked that. As their conversation drew to a close, Jo thought she caught a glimpse of a familiar-looking diagram as Matt flicked his notebook shut.

11

"So, how did it go?"

Edward and Matt were back in the comfy velvet chairs in *their* meeting place. It was a dreary day and raining out-side—the bay window was steamed up from the combination of steam from the coffee machine and the combined warmth from the people taking shelter from the miserable weather. A hot chocolate worked wonders for the soul on days like these.

"It went well, I was really pleased," said Matt enthusiasti-cally. "Jo gave me a really clear idea of what she expected from me. I made copious notes while we were talking, and I'm pretty sure that I can put a lot of what she mentioned into action fairly immediately. Yeah, it was really helpful." Matt had his notebook open on the table and Edward could see the results of the conversation.

"That sounds great—you were lucky with Jo, though."

"What do you mean?" Matt looked puzzled.

"Well, many managers will have their niche expectations, but they will be intuitive to them, and they often haven't given them conscious thought before—you're lucky, because Jo clearly has given it some thought." Edward smiled to himself.

"What should I have done if Jo hadn't given her niche expectations some thought?"

"Well, that does make life a little trickier," said Edward, "but by no means impossible. Some managers may be caught by surprise when you ask that question, others may feel intimidated by the fact you are asking for something that they may not have given conscious thought to: you've caught them off guard, and they may feel threatened by that. So, use your knowledge of them to consider how best to manage the situation. If it's clear that you've caught them off guard, then I find that asking them the question 'What's most important to you in our working together?' is a good way of initiating the conversation. You can always ask them to consider what their niche expectations might be, and then schedule another time to meet, so as to give them some time in which to collect their thoughts."

Matt was nodding as he made notes in his notebook.

Edward continued: "If they get really stuck, you could offer some suggestions to them, based on what you have observed seems to pique their interest. That may be the quality of written reports, dress code, time keeping, or keeping them informed of things, for example. You can then have a discussion around your suggestions. This often prompts them to come up with additional points as they dig up some of their unconscious, intuitive expectations. As I said, you were lucky though with Jo—she's given this some pre-thought. But you might want to consider other strategies for the future—Jo won't be your manager for ever."

"That's a good point, I've not considered that, but you're right. Jo has done well, and I'm sure she'll move on again in the future. Am I wasting my time, then, getting to know all this stuff—shouldn't I wait until she moves on, and then start afresh with my new boss?"

Edward was surprised at Matt's uncharacteristically negative response.

Clarify their expectations
—ask your boss: "What's
most important to you
in our working together?"

"No. Because you will be relying on Jo to give her successor positive feedback about you—so that you start off your relationship with them seeing you as someone who is an asset to the department, and who adds real value. The sooner you start matching or, even better, *exceeding*, Jo's expectations of you, in every sense, then the sooner you build up a positive profile in her mind. There's no time to waste!"

Matt smiled, "You're right, sorry."

Edward smiled reassuringly, and gave his mentee a second to regain his positive focus.

Edward sat back in his chair. "How are you doing? All this making sense?"

"Absolutely—I've got a clear sense of the three dimensions of expectations—I know what the organization expects of me—*Our Behaviors*—I know what the expectations are for my role; and I also know what personal—or niche—expectations my boss has of me in working with her. All I have to do now is make sure that I bear these things in mind and make small adjustments to what I do, and how I do it, in order to meet these expectations. So yes—in good shape I think—I feel like you've taken off my blindfold, Edward—I know what I'm aiming for, now!" Matt laughed.

"Good—it does sound like it all makes sense to you. You've now got a solid foundation on which you can build your future success. You know what's expected of you—you just need to make sure that you achieve or, even better, *exceed*, those expectations."

"Don't worry about that—you can take that as read," said Matt.

"OK, good—because now you can pay attention to the other four elements of career helium—the elements that are really going to fuel your rise through the organization. Think of a balloon as the metaphor for your career."

Edward continued: "The balloon needs fuel to get off the ground, right, just like your career does. The more helium you put into the balloon, the higher the balloon rises. Similarly, the more attention you pay to managing the elements that fuel your career—career helium—the higher your career will rise."

"That makes sense. So when do I learn about the other four elements?" asked Matt enthusiastically.

Edward gave a wry smile. "Soon."

Matt joined the Monday-morning team meeting. This was something that Jo had introduced about a year ago—it was her opportunity to get everyone fired up for the week ahead, and to make sure that everyone was aware of any "hot topics" for that week—perhaps promotions, changes in policy, or announcing new sales incentives. Matt liked the meetings—it was good to get together with everyone, and it gave him a framework for his week.

This morning's meeting was different, though. Natalie from Jasper's team had had her 21st birthday party over the weekend, and there was a lot of giggling and story swapping before Jo started the meeting. Matt also noticed that there was a new face in the room.

"Morning everyone—hope you all had a good weekend." There was giggling from some quarters, as Jo looked at the "party corner."

"We have a busy week ahead of us—it's month end and we are 10 percent below budget, so we need everyone to really focus on the phones this week—take a look at your own P&L and see where you could make up some ground for the team. Remember that we have the spa weekend up for grabs—so there's plenty to play for. Just to make it a really special weekend—I'm including a chauffeur to take you there and back if we can meet target by Wednesday."

There was a rumble of excitement from the team—it was clear that Jo was in "motivating" mode. Matt watched and learnt—he enjoyed watching the nuances of Jo's behavior as she ran these meetings—firm and always focused on the sales figures. She seemed to have a clear idea of what motivated the group. She was a good role model.

"And some of you may notice that there's a face in the room that you may not recognize." At that moment, the man got up from the desk that he was leaning against, smiled gently and joined Jo's side. She smiled and introduced him.

"This is Rich Peterson. He's going to be shadowing me for a few weeks, because ..." she paused, "I've been given a promotion and will be leaving in two weeks, so I'm going to be showing Rich the ropes. He'll be taking over from me when I leave."

The group broke into spontaneous applause, and Jo blushed a little. Mutterings of "she's done so well" rippled through the group.

Matt's heart sunk. He had worked so hard over the last few weeks since his previous meeting with Edward in making sure that he was doing everything that Jo had listed as her niche expectations, and he had been receiving some good feedback from her. She hadn't given him any hint that she might be leaving any time soon. He was disappointed, because he liked working with Jo, but he was also a little annoyed—had the last few weeks been a waste of time?

Rich introduced himself to the group, and gave a short synopsis of his experience and career: he had transferred from another sales division, which had been very successful, and his remit was to accelerate the growth that Jo had started, whilst she took a further step up the career ladder and became the Country Sales Manager, responsible for the whole of the UK sales operation. This was an impressive move—the UK was the largest sales operation in Europe, and second in the company only to the parent US operation. Jo was certainly doing well.

The group disbanded back to their desks and Jo began walking Rich around the sales floor, introducing him to each of the Sales Managers in turn.

"Congratulations, Jo," said Matt as she and Rich finally reached his desk.

"Thanks—I'll be sorry to leave the team, but onward and upward, Matt!"

That phrase triggered an intense déjà vu feeling in Matt's mind—he had heard that exact phrase somewhere before.

He quickly shook the thought from his head. "Absolutely," he replied, as he reached to shake his new boss's hand.

"I hear you're keen to make it to Sales Manager," said Rich by way of introduction.

Matt looked a little taken aback, "Yes. That's right."

"Well, I've got a pretty focused remit to achieve with you guys, so I'll be looking for people to work with me and step up to the challenge. Are you up for that, Matt?" Rich looked at Matt expectantly.

"Oh, definitely—looking forward to it!"

Rich and Jo smiled at each other, suggesting that they had already spoken about Matt and that they had somehow colluded to give Matt this opportunity.

"Excellent—glad to hear it. Well, I want to invest some time getting to know all my key people in the team, Matt, and Jo tells me that you are ambitious—so how about we get to know each other and I can share some of my plans with you. How does that sound?"

"That sounds like a great idea," beamed Matt.

"OK—I'll get Sophie to arrange a time for us to go and have a spot of lunch and we can get to know each other." Rich smiled and nodded his head slightly, signifying that the conversation had finished.

The two men shook hands, and Jo moved Rich on to meet the other sales teams.

Rich seemed like a good guy, and was certainly focused on getting the results that he had been charged with achieving. Matt recognized that he had been placed in a positive position by Jo—so the time that he had invested in understanding her expectations of him had created the positive impression that he was aiming for. He was in a good starting position with Rich, but he had understood career helium enough to know that he wouldn't be the only person in the sales team keen to get to know Rich so that they could deliver for him. Matt knew that the other elements of career helium that Edward had yet to share with him would be invaluable. He needed Edward. He needed him now.

Matt discovered that he had no contact details for Edward. He had met him by chance, and they had always arranged their next meeting when they were together. Matt made more visits to Starbucks than usual over the next few days, hoping to bump into Edward. He was concerned: Sophie had arranged his meeting with Rich on Friday, meaning that he had only two days to find his mentor.

What was he to do? Matt stood outside Starbucks and leant against the brick wall, gazing into the crowd. It was a warm spring day and he enjoyed the mild breeze for a moment as he let his mind wander.

Suddenly, he caught sight of something amongst the crowd—a brown linen suit with a large lime green check bobbed in and out of sight. This eccentric dress stood out in this part of the city and could mean only one thing. Matt's suspicions were correct. He had found what he was searching for.

He shook Edward's extended hand. "Hello there," the older man said with a broad grin on his face, his white goatee stretching as he smiled. "Lovely day, isn't it?"

"It certainly is," Matt replied with relief in his voice.

"What on earth's up with you dear boy?" asked Edward

"I was worried I wasn't going to ..." Matt paused, "Oh, never mind about that. I'm really pleased to see you!"

"Ditto," Edward responded and nodded toward the door of the coffee shop. "Shall we go inside?"

"Something cold today, I think, don't you?"

The two men ordered iced lattes, and after finding that "their" chairs were taken, decided to go outside. They found a modern-looking bench that looked a lot more uncomfortable that it actually was, and sat.

They both took a sip of their drinks. It wasn't long before Matt got down to business.

"Edward, I really need your help with something."

"Oh really?"

"I've got a new boss!" exclaimed Matt.

"Oh. You will need my help then! I did say that Jo wouldn't be around for ever."

"Well yes, you did, but I didn't think that she would be moving on quite so quickly!"

"Some things are out of your control, young man, and even career helium can't change that. But, you can easily put the elements of career helium to work with Rich, so you haven't wasted your time. Rather think of it as practice."

"I didn't say my new boss's name was Rich, did I?"

Edward looked sheepish for a split second. "Oh, you must have done. Anyway that's not important. I guess you want to learn about the other elements so that you can enlist his support in moving your career forward."

Matt felt a little confused. He was sure that he hadn't mentioned Rich's name to Edward. How had he known that?

This wasn't the first time that he had been distracted by Edward. Matt still couldn't place him—he had a nagging feeling that he recognized his face from somewhere. He put all of this to the back of his mind—Matt had too much to learn to allow himself to become distracted by the mystery of his mentor, he needed to learn more about the secret of career helium.

"It seems that I'm starting from a good position with Rich. Jo has painted me in a positive light and I want to make sure that I capitalize on that. He's taking me out for lunch in a couple of days' time to get to know me and talk through his plans—and I want to make sure that I get as much value from that meeting as possible. It's such a perfect opportunity to get to know him and lay the foundations of a solid relationship."

"Listen to you," said Edward smiling, "You've really taken all this on board. You would never have said that a few months ago, before I shared the secret of career helium with you."

"I know—I almost can't believe it myself, to be honest. I'm looking at situations differently, and seeing opportunity where I had never seen it before. So you see that I need your help so that I can make the most of this lunch with Rich." Matt's tone held just a hint of desperation.

"Oh, I certainly do see, yes." Edward drained his iced latte and placed the cup on the floor. He reached for his Smythson journal, and Matt knew that the lesson was about to begin.

14

"What's the first thing you have to do when you meet with Rich?" asked Edward.

"Well, I guess I need to talk through *his* expectations, like I've done with Jo previously," replied Matt confidently.

"Well, yes, you will need to do that, but before that you should give him a potted history of who you are. Your background, the jobs that you have had before this one, that kind of thing, so that you make sure that he has accurate information about you. It sounds like Jo has given him an overview of who you are—but there's only one way to make sure that she has covered all the points that you think are most important ..." Edward paused mid-sentence and looked at Matt expectantly.

"... And that's for me to tell him myself!" Matt said with little hesitation.

"Exactly—because that way, you can emphasize the part of your career history or background that *you* think is most important. There's only one person who can really do you justice—and that's you."

"Absolutely," replied Matt confidently. "And, after that— then I discuss his expectations of my role, and also try to get a sense of his personal, niche expectations?"

"Yes, definitely—and this is more important with a new boss, because they will be enthusiastic and focused, and looking for allies. Giving them an opportunity to share their plan with you, giving your support, and ascertaining how you should work best together is quite a powerful combination, and will be very attractive to Rich."

"When you put it like that, I see what you mean," said Matt, pausing for second.

What his mentor had told him made perfect sense, and gave him a perspective that he hadn't previously considered.

"I have already been through that process with Jo, so I'm pretty confident that I can manage that conversation well," said Matt.

"Good—having done it before, you will find it easier than you may have done the first time. But remember—you'll need to go through this process of clarifying the three dimensions of expectations whenever you get a new boss," said Edward.

"I understand that—although let's hope that Rich will be around for a while!"

Edward smiled. "Well I hope so, but things move so quickly these days—it's difficult to predict."

Matt nodded. He had been working in the sales department for just over two years, and Rich was the third boss that he had had during that time, so he knew from experience that Edward was absolutely right.

"Well done Matt, you've taken Jo's leaving in your stride and you're all set to discuss expectations with your new boss. So—you're back on track."

Edward continued: "Now, there are five elements in career helium, two of which are focused around your boss, and three of which are focused on the broader environment in which you work." Edward opened his journal and the pages fell open at the career helium diagram. Clearly a well-thumbed page, it was almost as if the journal knew the way.

"We will move on to look at the elements of profile, networking, and politics later. The most immediate thing is to make sure that you are prepared for your lunch with Rich, and this gives you an excellent opportunity to explore the second element of career helium with him."

Matt had slipped comfortably into pupil mode, and was focused intently on Edward. He valued his support and guidance so much, and he wanted to make the most of each opportunity he had to learn from him.

"The second element of career helium is about understanding, managing, and facilitating your boss."

"What do you mean by *facilitating* my boss?" Matt asked. He'd heard the word used before, but never in this context.

"It simply means enabling your boss to achieve his goals. You are closer to the 'troops' than he is. Therefore you can act as a valuable ally by working from that position and using your influence with *them* to ensure that your boss achieves *his* goals."

"Oh I see. Clever!" exclaimed Matt.

"Well, maybe, but your position could actually be as powerful to him as his is to you—he will need to reach out to his staff, and you can help him do that. It's good to remember that. Achieving success is rarely done alone."

Matt thought about this for a few seconds. "You're right, the relationships that I have with my colleagues within the team will be valuable to him, particularly as he is new and the team will be unsure of him. If I talk positively about him, then that will help him greatly."

"Particularly as he settles in and creates his own profile and reputation with this new team, yes," added Edward.

Achieving success
is rarely done alone.

"OK, so how do I," Matt paused and consulted his notes to make sure that he got the exact phrasing right, "go about understanding, managing, and facilitating my boss?"

Edward smiled. He was touched by the studious approach that Matt was taking.

"It's an extension of the approach you took when we were talking about expectations—this time, you are getting to know what the expectations are that are placed on your boss from others. Remember—he has a boss too. Now, managers rarely share this naturally with their team members, but by having this information, you will be able to consider ways in which you could consciously enable them to achieve their goals and objectives. The more you can help and support them to achieve their goals, the more they will appreciate you, and be motivated to help and support you, in your own quest for success."

"Makes sense—but how do I actually *do* that?" Matt furrowed his brow.

Although the concept genuinely made sense to him, this was an unusual way of looking at his relationship with his boss, and he had no idea how to make it happen. He eagerly awaited guidance from Edward.

"This," said Edward, pausing, "is a delicate operation. That's why I'm going to give you a structure to use to gather that information. Don't worry—it's pretty straightforward and you can easily use it. But I would suggest that you stick to it: going 'off piste' on this element could create the wrong type of impression with your boss."

"What do you mean?"

"Well, first, you need to bear in mind that you must start from a position of mutual trust with your boss for this conversation to be an effective one. You will be asking him to be open with you, and he will need to feel comfortable enough with you to be able to do that. He needs to know that you are trustworthy and are not going to abuse the trust and confidence that he is placing in you. Second, you will be asking him to share information with you that he probably doesn't share with most people openly. So, to make sure that you don't delve into areas that aren't necessary—and which will distract your discussions with him from *your* aim—you should stick to the structure. If you don't, you risk portraying yourself as being nosey or manipulative—and that's not a good place to be coming from, particularly when you are getting to know each other."

"Oh, definitely—I don't want that at all—that would be career suicide." Matt contemplated what Edward was sharing with him for a moment.

"You've got me feeling worried about this, Edward," he continued.

"There's no need at all to feel worried, Matt. As long as you are focused on the outcome you want from these discussions, and you follow the structure, you'll get the information that you are looking for, and demonstrate your commitment to your boss and his cause. You will also gather information that will give you fuel for your career. Everyone wins."

"OK, so what's the structure?" Matt wanted the detail.

"Well, there are four stages. I call them the '4Ps'—it makes it easier to remember them that way."

Edward reached into his jacket pocket and unclipped his Montblanc pen. He smoothed a fresh page in his journal, and turned towards Matt.

Edward wrote the following words on the page in front of him:

Personality
Purpose & Plan
Pay
Profile

Matt copied each of them down in his own notepad as the words flowed from the nib of Edward's pen.

"Now, there are a few ground rules to bear in mind before you can use this structure," said Edward, with a note of caution in his voice.

"First, you can gather some of the information that you need from your own knowledge of your boss—each stage does not necessarily need to be *discussed*," Edward emphasized.

"Second, you may need to take a medium-term approach to gathering all the information that you need. Your boss may not talk about some of this stuff unless he feels comfortable with you—and you are the best person to evaluate the level of your trust. Let your intuition, your gut instinct, lead you on this one."

Matt nodded as he wrote.

"And, finally, *don't* have a specific meeting set aside to discuss this with your boss. Instead, integrate the discussion about these 'Ps' into a variety of different conversations with him. What I mean is that you shouldn't have the '4Ps' as a point on one of your meeting agendas. Instead, take a conversational approach to gathering this information—it is more subtle. Of course, it will mean that it might take longer to gather all the information that you need, but the process tends to work better that way. Which is why I said that you should focus on the medium term for this."

"The first P is for *Personality*. Now, your boss is like anyone else in your life—the longer you know him, the more you

Understanding your boss:

- Personality
- Purpose & Plan
- Pay
- Profile

learn about him. And the more you learn about him, the deeper your knowledge of him, and what makes him tick, grows. With this knowledge, you are able to refine the way that you interact with him, and make these interactions even more effective."

"What sort of things do you mean?" asked Matt.

"Everyone is different, Matt, and everyone works in a different way. To some people, being organized and detail driven is very important, yet to others it isn't. Some people value creativity, to others it's not important at all. If you understand what makes your boss tick, in a work sense, you can always make sure that you pay particular importance to this when you are doing something for him."

Matt looked a little puzzled. Edward continued.

"Let me give you an example. I like to work in quite a creative way—I'm always looking for new and different ways of doing things. However, one boss I worked with I remember, didn't value creativity. He was a real detail person—so he would always find that spelling mistake or inaccuracy in a document or report that I had produced for him. I would have read it beforehand of course, but I'm just not tuned in to that—so I would often miss things."

"I can imagine he didn't like that very much!" laughed Matt.

"No, he didn't," smiled Edward, "so you know what I did? I made sure that whenever I prepared a report for him, I would print it out, find somewhere quiet, and go through the report, making sure that I read every word, rather than just skimming through it as I had done before. The result was that I satisfied this need for detail from my boss, and he grew to value me more and more—because I appeared to work in a way that he valued."

"Ah, I see," said Matt, nodding. "You knew that detail was important to him, so you made a conscious effort to focus on it, because to not do that would frustrate your boss, and he wouldn't value you."

"Exactly," said Edward, nodding. "That's exactly right. His view of me wouldn't erode overnight, of course, but I quickly picked up on what was important, and so I forced myself to pay particular attention to it."

"Clever," said Matt.

"Perhaps, but I'd like to think of it more as just being sensible—the more you can work, or *appear* to work, in a similar way to your boss, the better."

The subtle emphasis that Edward had placed on the word "appear" wasn't lost on Matt. In the short time that he had known Edward he had picked up on the fact that making career helium work didn't mean that Matt had to change as a person—he just had to pay attention to things that had been there all along, but that he perhaps hadn't focused on before. He thought of the many times that Jo had been frustrated with him for not filing his monthly sales results on time. He thought that placing priority on spending time on the phone during the busy time was more important. He didn't realize that there would be a greater payoff for him in the long run if he invested more time in taking care to give Jo his monthly report by the deadline that she had set. He felt frustrated as he looked back and thought of the many opportunities that he had missed to build his professional relationship with Jo.

"Now, there's more to this," continued Edward.

"We've talked about what's important to your boss in terms of his work personality, his work style; but there is also his true personality."

"You mean what he is like as a person?"

The more you can work, or _appear_ to work, in a similar way to your boss, the better.

"Yes, but also all other aspects of his personal life. For example, how his family unit is made up, whether he has kids or not, what he likes to do on holiday, whether he has any great interests—you know, that sort of thing," said Edward.

"Right, I know what you mean, but why would knowing if he was a golfer or not, matter?"

Edward was touched by Matt's apparent naivety.

"OK, let's forget your boss for a second. Who's your best friend?"

Matt was a little puzzled by this question, which seemed out of context, but indulged Edward with an answer. "Simon," he said.

"OK, tell me about him," Edward prompted.

"Well, we met at school, we took a lot of classes together. He and I both like science fiction so we go to the cinema together quite a lot, and then we have this thing where we go to the Pizza Hut around the corner afterwards and talk about the film ..." Edward stopped him mid-sentence.

"So, you have similar interests?"

"Most of the time, yes." Matt still wasn't sure where Edward was taking his line of questioning.

"Well, I'm going to bet that as you found out more about each other, and discovered that you had more in common, you grew closer and your relationship developed into what it is today."

"I guess so, yes."

"Well—think of your bosses in the same way. The more you get to know about them, the more opportunity you have for finding those things in common that connect you both together. People need to have some reason to bond, Matt, and people gravitate toward those that they feel are most like them."

Matt paused for a second. "So, I should spend some time getting to know my boss on a personal level, is that what you are saying? How is that going to help me?"

People need to have some reason to bond. People gravitate toward those that they feel are most like them.

"In two ways. It may be that you have a shared interest—giving you an opportunity to bond over something. It doesn't matter what it is—it could be a shared interest in fly-fishing, it's not important." Matt smiled—he didn't imagine Rich had any interest in anything even remotely resembling fly-fishing.

Edward continued. "The important thing is that, over time, as you get to know your boss, you will discover things that you have in common. Leverage these to build a closer relationship with him. You'll be surprised at the impact that these conversations could have on your boss's perception of you."

"Actually, come to think of it, as you'd expect, there is a fair amount of gossip in the office at the moment about Rich. Someone said that he raced bikes at an amateur competitive level at the weekend, and I'm in the process of taking lessons to learn how to ride a motorbike as I've always wanted one."

"There you go. Perfect!" exclaimed Edward, slapping his leg with the palm of his hand. Matt smiled—he was pleased that he had already identified a leverage point for developing a relationship with his new boss.

"Now, some bosses share personal information about themselves very rarely—so always be aware. Make sure that you don't miss any opportunity to learn more about what's important to your boss—either in terms of working style or from a personal point of view," Edward continued.

Matt nodded.

Edward noticed that Matt had written some notes in his notebook under the heading of "Next meeting with Rich."

"What's that?" he asked, pointing at the notes.

"Oh, I'm just making a list as we go along of things to make sure that I talk to Rich about when we meet later this week," said Matt innocently.

"That's what I thought. But, Matt, it doesn't work like that.

Gathering this information is something that you need to do gently, subtly—you need to tease the information out of your boss over time. If you approach the '4Ps' as simply an 'agenda item,' they will think that you are pumping them for information, or just being plain nosey—and neither of those approaches will win you many friends. Timing is everything."

Edward was right. Matt was disappointed that he hadn't understood that. "Sorry—you're right, I guess I was a little too focused."

"That's OK," smiled Edward, "I appreciate you now understand the power of having information like this and you just want to use it as quickly as possible, but the timing and the approach you take are both really important here.

"Now, one thing you *can* do in a meeting, is this ..." Edward circled the second P on his list: "Purpose."

"You remember the conversation we had about clarifying the expectations of your boss?" asked Edward.

"Of course."

"Well—your boss will be having a similar conversation with *his* boss, and *his* boss will be having the same conversation with *his* boss, and so on—up the chain."

Matt hadn't thought of that before, but Rich's manager would have expectations of him, just the way that Rich would have expectations of Matt. He laughed.

"I've never thought of it like that before, Edward, but you're absolutely right!"

"So what does that mean for you?" Edward wanted to see if Matt could work out the basis of the second P himself.

"Well, if Rich has had that conversation with his boss about what he needs to achieve, then that means that if I ask him, he will have a pretty clear and conscious view of his objectives."

"Absolutely, and how are you going to do that?" Edward's

eyes flicked briefly to the list that Matt had written under the heading "Next meeting with Rich" that the two had discussed just minutes before.

"I would discuss it with Rich in a meeting." Matt was speaking very slowly, and looking for some reaction from Edward as he answered him, as confirmation that he was on the right lines. Edward nodded, giving him the confirmation he was looking for.

"Absolutely," he beamed. Edward was pleased with his young protégé. "You can legitimately have a conversation with your boss about his objectives—provided that you explain that the more you know about what's expected of *him*, the more you can ensure *your* contribution underpins his purpose."

"Kind of 'help me to help you'?" asked Matt.

"Exactly like that. And what boss is going to turn that offer down? It shows that you have given thought to your relationship, and that you are explicitly pledging your support to your boss, which will serve to develop and deepen your relationship with him still further."

"I can see that that would be very appealing." Matt scribbled in his notebook.

Edward continued, "Of course, once you have had this explicit conversation, and committed to support your boss in the achievement of his goals, you need to make sure that you make good your promise and do actively support him through your behavior, actions, and achievements. Otherwise, that will affect the trust between you."

Matt looked up from his notebook and pointed to the '4Ps': "Now, *Pay*, I don't understand that—I can't ask Rich how much he gets paid!"

Edward chuckled. "No, of course you can't—and the third P isn't about *what* they get paid—but rather *how* they get paid."

Help me to help you: ask about your boss's objectives—explicitly pledge your support to your boss and what he or she needs to achieve.

Now Matt was really confused.

"Er, well, straight into his bank account I would imagine, the same as me."

Edward rolled his eyes. "No, it doesn't mean that. The third P is about the *constitution* of your boss's compensation. If your boss is paid a straight salary, and he therefore has no way of influencing the amount he is paid, he may be less focused on exceeding the expectations that his boss places on him, compared to a boss who received a bonus that's linked to his or her performance. If Rich is paid on performance—i.e. the better the results his team achieves, the larger his bonus, then it will inevitably alter his perspective. Having someone like you pledging your support to him and enabling him to achieve his purpose through your own performance, will be very useful to him, Matt. This kind of support will contribute to higher team performance, which, in turn, will contribute to higher compensation for your boss."

"Ah, I see, I'd never thought of that before. So, it's therefore in his best interest to get me hooked into his objectives—because he can achieve them through me."

"Exactly—and your colleagues as well—you all contribute to it."

"I've never thought of it like that before."

"No, I don't suppose you have," replied Edward thoughtfully.

"Wow. And I guess that it's perfectly safe to talk to Rich about this openly—you know, in a meeting or something?"

"Well, yes, it would be, but actually you might not need to ask him. If you ask around gently, people may know how the Area Sales Managers get paid, particularly those Sales Managers in your area who might be looking to get promoted—I bet they've found that out!" Edward responded.

"Good point—I'll ask Jasper. I would have thought he'd be getting promoted pretty soon—he'll know."

"There you go—so you can get that information by asking others. You see what I mean—you can collect some of the information around the '4Ps' without asking your boss directly. Which means that you can keep your conversations with him focused on the specifics that you can't get from anyone else," said Edward.

Matt completed his notes on the pad in front of him.

"OK, so on to *Profile*." Edward was clearly keen to complete Matt's education on how to get the best out of his boss.

Matt flicked back to the career helium diagram that he had copied down during his first meeting with his mentor. "*Profile*—right, now didn't you mention that when you introduced me to the concept of career helium," said Matt, pointing at the diagram with his pen.

Edward responded. "Indeed. And we will be covering that later. Right now, we need to talk about your *boss's* profile. The two concepts are more or less the same—but the way in which you approach them will be different."

Matt wasn't sure that he understood, but he had learnt enough from his friend to realize that Edward would ensure that he did understand in good time. He trusted him, and so he focused on the fourth P, placing his faith in his teacher.

"So, as far as you are concerned, to put the fourth P into action, the question is this: Who does your boss need to influence in order to develop his own career?" Matt sat up and looked expectantly at Edward, hoping that the question was rhetorical.

He was relieved as Edward continued: "Because, in a similar way to you, your boss will have a few, select, people who will have the power to impact on his career. He needs to make sure that he keeps those people on side, that they are aware of his achievements, and that he works to develop his relationship with them. These people will want to see that he is doing a good job and getting the results that they expect, in the way that they expect. Now, you need to understand who these people are, so that whenever you have any interaction with them, you can make sure that it is positive, and therefore reflects well on your boss."

"What do you mean?" asked Matt. He really wasn't sure how he could influence these people who would be so much more senior than him.

"Well, you are your boss's representative in everything that you do. Everything that you do, and how you do it, is a reflection on him."

"I see," reflected Matt.

"Everything, no matter how small and seemingly insignificant, reflects on your boss," Edward repeated.

Matt was unnerved by Edward's emphasis—he wanted to check his understanding.

"What do you mean?" he asked.

"Exactly what I said. First of all, you need to know *with whom* it's important that your boss has a positive profile. Edward did not want to spoon-feed Matt.

"Now, how will you find that out?"

"Well, I could guess a few people—Rich's boss, and probably his boss's boss. Also, he would want to show Jo that he could take what she had started and develop it further, and then there would be a few of his peers who are managing other teams that he would also want to have a positive profile with." Matt smiled. He was surprised, but pleased, that he was able to answer Edward's question.

"Good. I would say that that was pretty accurate. Few

people know about the secret of career helium, and as a result, few people give conscious thought to developing their profile at work. So, sometimes if you ask your boss to list the people that he needs to build a strong profile with, he may well be embarrassed that he doesn't have an answer. Oftentimes, if you know how the organization works, and you understand how your boss fits into the structure, it is likely that you can work out for yourself who your boss's key stakeholders are." That made sense to Matt—after all, he had been able to correctly identify Rich's stakeholders for Edward at a moment's notice.

Sensing Matt's understanding of this, Edward continued: "Now that you know who your boss's stakeholders are, you can make sure that any and every interaction you have with them paints your boss in a positive light."

"Can you give me an example of what you mean?" asked Matt.

"Sure. Every time you meet one of Rich's stakeholders in the corridor, be warm and welcoming. Whenever you have a chance to attend a meeting to talk about what your team is doing—grab the opportunity, and present a positive and motivating picture. If you are asked to do something, anything, for one of Rich's stakeholders, seize the moment and do it, and do it well. If you bump into one of his stakeholders at the coffee machine, or in the line at the sandwich bar, have just one positive success story prepared that you can tell them about the broader team. Don't be pushy or overenthusiastic. The key words here are true, sincere, and authentic. Do it because you believe it, and you want to be a supportive messenger about your boss's team."

Matt nodded enthusiastically. "And I guess that the authenticity is really important?"

"Definitely." Edward's eyes widened as he gave his reply. "This isn't about sucking up—that's sycophantic and transparent. This is about being mature, confident, and appreciating the importance of being a positive representative for your boss."

"I see that—it's one of those longer-term strategies again, isn't it—help him to help me?" asked Matt.

"That's exactly what it is, yes. If you make sure these small instances and interactions place a positive light on your boss and his team, over time these small occasions add up to create a positive profile in the minds of your boss's stakeholders—that's what you are aiming for. This is subtle, but over time, it's effective. This is your investment in your boss, and therefore an investment in yourself," said Edward.

"OK—I get it. In fact, looking back, I can think of several opportunities that I've missed. I know just the kind of thing that you mean, Edward." And, with that, Matt jotted some thoughts of his own in his pad alongside the notes that were inspired by his mentor.

There was silence between the two men for a moment, as they both reflected on what they had discussed.

"I can't tell you how insightful and helpful this is for me, Edward."

"Good, I'm glad. You do seem to be getting the hang of it. Now, remember what I said earlier—this structure works, so follow it as it is—but do give thought to which aspects of the '4Ps' that you may know already, or could get from sources other than your boss."

"I will, thanks, yes, I've got that."

"Great. So, you feel more relaxed and confident about your meeting with Rich later this week?" asked Edward.

"Oh, I can't tell you—I'm so pleased that I found you! Now,

Appreciate the importance of being a positive representative for your boss.

I can make the most of my first meeting with Rich—I'm all set to make a good first impression."

"Well, you never get a second chance to make one of those!"

The two friends laughed. "Absolutely!" said Matt.

The lunch with Rich went well. Matt was surprised at how open and honest his new boss was, and how much he appeared to know about Matt, and both his recent disappointment and his aspirations for the future. Jo had clearly briefed him well, and Rich made it clear to Matt that he would coach and support him toward his promotion in exchange for his support and his dedication to results. It seemed like a good deal. Matt was pleased when Rich shared with him his remit for his new job—it allowed him to mentally tick off one of the "4Ps" that Edward had introduced him to, and was his secret agenda for the meal: Rich's *Purpose & Plan* was clear.

Later that day, Matt reflected on the conversation that he had had with Rich—and how he had put his knowledge of career helium into practice. During the lunch, he had found that he was able to gather a significant amount of the information he was looking for from his new boss, simply by letting the natural conversation take its course. Just as Edward had predicted, Rich needed and wanted to secure Matt's support. Rich needed focused and committed people around him to enable him to achieve his own objectives, so it was in his own best interest to make sure that he took this opportunity to get to know his new colleague, and to make sure that he secured Matt's engagement to his *Purpose & Plan.* Matt's interest in motorbikes captured Rich's attention and gave Matt the opportunity he was looking for to secure some connection with Rich's *Personality. Matt placed another tick against his mental checklist.*

Before joining Rich for lunch, Matt had made a point of meeting Jasper for a coffee, and had asked him how his new boss would be compensated. Jasper, who was always in the know about these things, confirmed Matt's suspicion that Rich would be in line for a bonus of anything up to 40 percent of his salary if he could achieve the targets that he was being set. Clearly, Rich would therefore place significant value on anyone who would help him to achieve his goals, and Matt knew that if he could establish a relationship with Rich, and demonstrate his support through his performance, then this placed him in a very strong position. This knowledge of the third P, *Pay*, meant that Matt could avoid discussing it with Rich directly, which he wasn't keen to do, whilst securing the knowledge he was looking for about the last outstanding "P."

Matt flicked back through his notebook and looked at the constituent elements of career helium. He smiled to himself as he realized that he had placed himself in an extremely strong position with his new boss within a very short space of time. He had quickly recovered the ground that he felt he had lost with Jo's sudden departure, and had already put the first two elements of career helium into play with Rich. He was pleased with himself and with the progress that he was making.

He shook his head gently as he sat back in his chair and considered the positive impact that his accidental discovery of career helium had had on him. He had known of it for barely a month and already he had demonstrably changed the way in which he approached both his work and his relationship with his boss. It all seemed so simple, sensible, and straightforward; he found it difficult to remember how he had approached work before meeting his mentor.

One thing was certain, he thought: he had made significant inroads with his new boss, and wanted to make sure he leveraged this opportunity. He looked at the career helium sketch in front of him and was reminded of one thing: there were three elements that he hadn't yet learned about and if they were anything like as powerful as the first two, he wanted to learn about them, and learn about them quickly. This meant only one thing. He needed to find Edward.

"I take the development of my team very seriously." Rich was addressing his team leaders at the Monday-morning meeting. This was the first one that Rich had hosted since Jo had introduced him to the team, and no one was really sure what to expect. Except Matt.

"I want to get a clear sense of the skills that we have in the team, and how I can support your ongoing development so that you can all reach your potential," Rich continued, "and so, I have asked Suzy to join us from Human Resources. Suzy is going to be taking us all through a self-development 360-degree feedback process, which will give you all an opportunity to gather some confidential feedback about yourself and your working style from your colleagues within the team, and also some of your peers and senior colleagues. I place a high importance on open and honest feedback—and there's no better place to start than by getting some of that feedback on yourself."

Rich introduced Suzy, who proceeded to explain how the exercise would work in practice. Essentially Matt would nominate people to give him feedback, the information would be collated under themes and then he would get a copy of the resulting report, which summarized all the feedback. Rich would get a copy, and he would use this to determine the key skills and potential contribution of everyone in his team. He could then decide how to leverage those skills to the best advantage of the team.

The "old" Matt would have seen this as a negative intrusion. The "old" Matt would question the benefits when all he really placed importance on was achieving his sales targets every month and keeping his sales team motivated. Now, however, he looked at this situation with a fresh, different, and more positive approach. Matt recognized that this would be an opportunity to get some hard facts on what others thought of him, and allow him a further opportunity to discuss himself and his career with Rich.

This could only be a good thing, he decided.

Matt had made his way outside to buy the breakfast that he had missed in his rushed journey to work that morning, and was crossing the road when he heard the screech of tires behind him. He turned to see a taxi, with the passenger scrambling to roll down the window.

"Hello there!"

Matt smiled. "Hello Edward—are you off somewhere?"

"No—*we* are!" he said with a twinkle in his eye. "Hop in."

Matt laughed. "I can't—I've only come out to get coffee and a muffin!"

"Of course you can—take your lunch hour early—c'mon, this won't take long. I've got something to show you."

Matt rolled his eyes. He couldn't believe that he was doing this. But Edward's charm was irrefutably persuasive. He opened the door of the taxi and jumped in.

"So where are we going?"

"You'll see!"

Matt laughed and shook his head. "I don't believe I'm doing this!" he said.

"Oh, I think you do!" replied Edward with a broad and beaming smile. "Now, sit back and enjoy the ride."

The black cab weaved its way through London's streets,

and after a short time it pulled up somewhere in the city that Matt didn't recognize.

Edward took Matt by the arm. "Come with me," he said, leading the young man in the direction of an old and disused building. It had old-fashioned gold writing above the door, which suggested that it may have been some kind of shop at some stage in its history. The worn and dusty shop front stood out from the others around it like a sore thumb. It certainly didn't fit the character of the area, and didn't even appear to be open. This was a crowded part of the city but everyone seemed to be walking past the shop front as if it didn't exist. No one even appeared to notice it. It was quite strange. Matt was cautious.

Edward stood in the doorway, turned a key in the dusty lock, and pushed open the door with his shoulder. He beckoned his young friend to join him. "Come along, Matt, there's nothing to be worried about."

Matt smiled, if a little nervously, and joined his friend. The interior and exterior of the building couldn't have been more of a contrast. Inside were balloons of different shapes, sizes, and colors filling every space. They were everywhere. They hung in bundles from the ceiling, they spilled out from large cardboard boxes stacked in the corner, they even covered the floor, making the old and well-worn floorboards barely visible. The two men had to kick them out of the way to walk through what appeared to be some kind of workshop.

"What *is* this place?" asked Matt with a disbelieving grin on his face. The jollity of being surrounded by brightly colored balloons was infectious.

"It's great isn't it? I come here when I need to be reminded of something," replied Edward mysteriously.

"Reminded of what?"

The space inside the workshop seemed to go on and on—it was huge. The two men reached what appeared to be some kind of workstation, where tanks of gas were standing alongside balloons that were sitting limply in boxes waiting to be blown up.

Whether Edward hadn't heard Matt's question, or he chose to ignore it was unclear. Either way, he didn't answer it. He leant on the workstation, picked up a balloon, and began to stretch it.

"So—how did it go with Rich?"

Matt was taken aback. "Er, good, actually, thanks. I have put all your advice into practice, and I really feel that I'm in a very positive position with him. I'm glad that I bumped into you, though, because I want to make sure that I capitalize on what I've achieved so far and I really wanted to hear about the other three elements of career helium so I can put them to work as soon as possible."

Matt hoped that this would prompt Edward to share more of his secret with him.

Edward let the large red balloon that he was stretching snap onto his hand. He looked at Matt and paused for a second.

"OK, grab a seat!" he exclaimed suddenly.

Matt didn't need asking twice, and enthusiastically grabbed a stool at the workbench and pulled it closer to Edward.

"So, remind me, what are the three elements of career helium that we haven't looked at yet?" asked the older man.

Matt responded without hesitation: "Profile, Networking, and Politics."

"Good, very good. OK, you'll remember that I've explained that the first two elements of career helium are focused on your boss and your relationship with him, and the other three are focused on the broader environment in which you work?"

Matt nodded. "Well, we are going to make that switch now and focus on how you manage and interact within your broader work environment. I've encouraged you, until now, to focus on the relationships and expectations that are very obvious and close to you. From this point forward, I'll be asking you to take more of a step back, and to look at things from a more ..." Edward paused and looked briefly to the ceiling as if he was searching for the right word "... strategic perspective, if you will."

Matt shuffled on his stool. The words that Edward had chosen made him feel as if this was his organizational coming-of-age moment: the definitive moment when he would make a significant step forward in his career, as if he was leaving his organizational childhood behind and moving toward manhood. He unconsciously straightened himself on his stool, and cleared his throat. "OK, got it," he said, his voice taking on an unconsciously serious quality, in contrast with the rather colorful and jovial environment he found himself in.

"All three of these elements relate to each other—they are not separate entities. Remember that. They are also the three elements that will have the biggest potential payback for you. It's a unique skill to be able to develop and maintain a positive profile, to use networking to your advantage, and especially to manage the politics that exists within organizations. If you can do these three things well, then your success is assured."

This was exactly what Matt wanted to hear. He knew that these skills were new to him, but he was certain of one thing: he had seen the power of the two elements he had learned about so far, and if they were anything to go by, he was determined to understand the other three so he could reap the benefits as soon as possible.

"Now we are going to focus on *profile*—and that is why I have brought you here." Edward gestured to the balloons surrounding them. Matt sensed that he was getting closer to understanding why they were sitting in this rather unusual environment, and hoped that all would soon be revealed.

"I was wondering why you had brought me here—it is a little out of the ordinary!" exclaimed Matt.

"Yes, but sometimes it's good to put yourself in an environment that is unknown or unusual to you—somehow it brings more clarity." Edward sounded serious and Matt began to regret his light-hearted comment. He coughed nervously.

"Matt—what does *profile* mean to you?" Edward asked firmly.

The young man thought for a moment. "Er, I've not really thought about that before, I guess how well known you are?" He remembered one of the comments that Jo had made to him when she had explained that he hadn't been successful with the promotion panel. Edward was pleased with the answer.

"Yes, that's not bad—you're on the right lines."

The old man continued. "You remember when we first met, I said that if you really want to accelerate your progression, it's not your performance on the job alone that's going to get you there? You need to make sure that people know *who* you are, so that you are visible to them, and *what* you are doing, so your work is visible to them also. By developing a profile within your organization, you will make yourself visible to those that have the power to progress you toward your goals. You need to stand out from the others—and you can make that happen just by thinking differently about how you position yourself within your group."

By developing a profile,
you make yourself
visible to those that have
the power to progress
you toward your goals.

This idea piqued Matt's interest. "So how do I do that?" he asked.

"The concept of your *profile* is really a combination of three things."

Edward took a piece of paper from a pile that sat next to him at the workstation. He pulled his familiar Montblanc pen from his inside jacket pocket, and created three bullet points on the page in front of him.

He looked up at Matt. "You were almost there on one count, though. The first is about making sure you are known by the *right* people, and you're correct that this is perhaps the strongest and most obvious of these three factors." He moved his pen down the list he had written in front of him. "The second is your reputation, and the third is what you are known for, specifically. All three of these factors combine to form your profile." Matt nodded—this did make sense.

He had been caught off guard by Edward in the street and didn't have his notebook with him, so he reached for a piece of paper from the workstation, found a rather dog-eared pencil, and scribbled down some notes to capture what Edward had said.

"Now, there are very small differences between each of these three factors, but it's understanding and considering these nuances that is the important thing." He paused while Matt completed his notes.

"To achieve the best result with these three factors, you need to layer them on top of each other, allowing each 'layer' to support and benefit the next—think of them as building blocks, if that makes it easier. So, I'm going to explain them in reverse, so that you can understand how they need to work with each other."

Edward could see that he had captured Matt's full attention. There were a number of things that he loved about sharing the power of career helium with people, and he had shared it with many. It was this that he loved most—seeing the desire and enthusiasm in the eyes of his pupils. Many had gone on to achieve great things, and he took great pleasure in watching them as they achieved more and more, surpassing even their own expectations.

"OK Matt, let me ask you a question. Imagine that you are going shopping in the supermarket, and you are standing in the washing powder aisle. You want to buy the best powder that will clean your clothes thoroughly."

"OK."

"There is a choice of many different products that you could buy—some brand leaders, others for more specialist cleaning requirements, some with specific stain control, some packaged in eye-catching colors, others packaged in a trendy and stylish way—there's a lot of choice on the shelves. How do you decide which one to buy?"

"Matt thought for a moment. "Well, I'd think of what I needed it to do—and then I would check out the different products, and then select the one that was suited to achieving what I wanted."

Edward smiled warmly. "Excellent, absolutely, very good. You would evaluate each of the options, and then compare them with your original objective," he summarized.

Matt smiled. He liked the way that Edward would ask him a question about something fairly innocuous from real life and then directly parallel it with something that he wanted to illustrate within the work context. This made it easier to understand, somehow.

"Now imagine that you are a manager at work. You have

a specific problem, a project let's say, that you need solving—how would you go about selecting the right person for the job?"

"Well, I would take a similar approach to the one you've just described—I'd consider the skills that I was looking for, then I would think of all the people I knew in the business, and from that I'd be able to highlight the person that I thought had the right skills—and then I'd go and ask for their help on the project."

"Right again." Matt was pleased—this element was easy, he thought to himself.

"So, if one of the management team was going through that process at work, what do you think they would highlight as *your* unique skills or contribution? How would they categorize you, Matt?"

Matt felt like he had been ambushed. Perhaps this wasn't so easy after all. After a moment's thought, he replied rather meekly, "Gosh, I don't know exactly."

Edward could see that Matt was embarrassed that he couldn't think of anything, and touched the young man's arm in a gesture of reassurance. "It's OK—if you knew all the answers, you'd be doing all this already." This did make Matt feel a little better.

"That's the first thing about developing your profile—you need to know what I like to call your *unique differentiator* is—you need to know what you do differently to everyone else: what is it about you, your style, your approach that is valuable, or attractive, to others? What *differentiates* you in a *unique* way?" Edward let this sink in for a moment and then continued.

"Imagine you are one of those packets of washing powder on the supermarket shelves—you need to have something

Know your unique differentiator.

special, something different from the others so that someone will buy you." This made sense to Matt, and what Edward was telling him clicked into place.

"I get it—I need to identify what is special or different about the way that I achieve. I'll need to think about that," said Matt.

"That's fine—I would expect that. Think about your colleagues, start with those that do a similar job to you, and then consider other people that you know. Think about them as a whole—how would you describe their attitude to work, do they just do what's expected or do they go further. Do they achieve by telling people what to do or by engaging people? What are they particularly good at—good with figures, very detail oriented, or good at dealing with difficult people? Perhaps they have a particular skill for turning around teams that aren't working together as they should."

"OK, I see what you mean—let me give that some thought."

"You do that—you might want to take a little quiet time out to settle on what your unique differentiator is—but it's crucial that you know, because the other two factors in your profile will be structured around that, and will complement and support it. I'll leave you to think about that."

Matt had written down some initial thoughts about what his unique differentiator could be, and Edward sat in silence for a moment to allow Matt to capture all the raw ideas that were swirling around in his mind. He would need to give this some serious consideration. Matt looked up from his page once he had finished, and sighed gently. He smiled at Edward: "OK."

Edward took this as his signal to continue with Matt's education.

The older man pointed to the second bullet point in front of him.

"Let's move on and look at *reputation*. Do you know of anyone who has a reputation?" asked Edward. Matt was slightly surprised by the question. "Doesn't everyone have a reputation?" he asked.

"Indeed. Everyone does have a reputation—some may have a more visible or well-known reputation than others, but essentially everyone will have a reputation to a greater or lesser degree."

"So where do reputations come from?" asked Matt inquisitively.

"Reputation is essentially how an individual is collectively viewed by others." Matt took another piece of paper from the workstation and captured Edward's last sentence word for word.

"A person's reputation will include their unique differentiator that we talked about before, which is essentially *what* they are known for, and this is then layered with the collective view of their approach—i.e. *how* they achieve it—the way in which they go about getting things done. This is not just their style and approach to the work in hand, but also how they interact with the people they work with, and how they manage the environment that they are working in. And of course, consciously or unconsciously, *every* interaction we have with other people will have an impact, no matter how tiny, on us. Over time, the impressions of these interactions build up in people's minds to form a reputation."

"Right, and I guess if you have a positive and visible reputation, your profile follows suit?"

"Well, you need to know what your reputation is so you can layer the third factor on top of your reputation in order to develop a successful organizational profile" replied Edward.

Know your reputation: get to know how others see you.

Matt referred to the loose papers that he had in front of him. "Right, and the final layer was 'making sure you're known by the right people'?"

Even though he didn't understand how he could make this happen, he looked to Edward for some indication that he was right.

He was right. "Exactly. But how do you do that? How do you make sure that you are known by the right people?" asked Edward

"I have absolutely no idea!" laughed Matt "I was hoping you could tell me that!"

"OK I will!" replied Edward, with a confident smile.

"Let's start at the beginning—who *are* the right people?"

"Oh, I don't know!" exclaimed Matt, sounding a touch despondent. He hated it when Edward asked him these questions straight off—he was frustrated that he couldn't think through the answers for himself.

Edward smiled—this was something that people sometimes found difficult to grasp.

"The key word is *right*. The right people for you, may not be the right people for someone else. Who the right people are for you, depends on a number of things, but most importantly, it's those people who could have an impact on your career, both positively and negatively."

"Why negatively?" asked Matt. He didn't understand why that would be the case—wouldn't you want to avoid those people?"

"Have you heard the phrase 'keep your friends close, and your enemies closer'?" Edward asked. "You also have to think about those people who may—currently at least—view you in a less than positive light—and make sure that you influence them too. In fact, oftentimes, influencing them can be very beneficial to you in the long run. You certainly need to be focused on those people."

"So how do I decide who the right people are for me?"

"How do you fancy a nice cup of tea?" asked Edward, quite out of the blue.

"Er, yes, sure," said Matt cautiously.

"Good. Well while I go and make us a pot, why don't you make a list of all those people who you think could have an impact on your career. Think of everyone—colleagues, your boss, your boss's boss, peers who could also have the ear of your boss, that sort of thing. Don't think of what they may think of you at this stage—just list everyone."

"OK, I see." While Edward disappeared, Matt went to work on his list. He thought of all the people that he came into contact with during the week, he listed all his peers in the office, he listed the people that he came into contact with in other departments, and he listed all the people that he knew were on the promotion panel. By the time Edward had returned with a pot of tea and two mismatching cups and saucers on a rusty circular tray that had obviously been "borrowed" from a pub at some stage in the distant past, he had gathered a list of 15 people.

"How did you get on?" asked Edward, passing Matt his cup of tea. "Managed to find a few biscuits as well," he added, excitedly.

"Great—thanks," said Matt, taking a chocolate biscuit from the packet. "I've listed ..." he counted the number of people on his list, rattling through the numbers under his breath "... 15 people. Some of whom I have dealings with regularly, like Jasper and Tim, for example, and some that I don't really know, but who could have an impact on my career—like William, who is Rich's boss. I maybe see him, to talk to, once a month."

"That's fine, though—he would certainly have a significant

impact on your career. Rich would certainly have to influence him to get you promoted, wouldn't he?"

"Yes, that's true."

"OK, this is a good start." Edward took a mouthful of tea and found himself a fresh piece of paper from one of the nearby workstations.

He drew a square on the page in front of him and divided it with a cross to make four equal-sized boxes.

Matt sat in silence as Edward labeled the two axes. The horizontal axis was marked with the word *relationship*, with the vertical axis labeled *influence*. He completed the simple diagram before turning back to Matt.

"Now, you need to think of those people on your list who have influence on your career." Edward pointed with his pen to the *influence* axis. "This axis acts as a continuum: you place people at the top who you feel have a high level of influence on your career and, conversely, place people who have a low level of influence on your career at the bottom. The ends of the axis are extremes—so the higher you place someone, the higher their level of influence." Edward looked to Matt for some signal that this was making sense.

Matt nodded. "OK, got it."

Edward continued: "Similarly, the horizontal axis is a continuum for the level of relationship that you have with someone—the left side of the axis signifies the relative strength of that relationship, and weakness from the middle to the right-hand side. Again this acts as a continuum—so the strongest relationship would be placed at the far left-hand side of the axis."

"I see. And would I be right in thinking that each of these four areas here is a combination of both those aspects—influence and relationship?"

"You would be absolutely right!" replied Edward, pleased

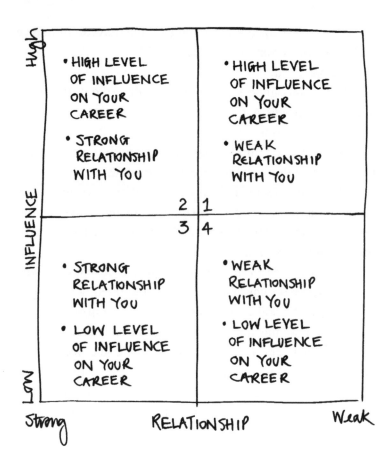

that his young protégé was thinking through what he was teaching him.

"Let me take you through each of these quadrants," said Edward, circling above the diagram with his sleek black pen.

Edward pointed to the quadrant in the top right-hand corner of the matrix. "People that you place in this quadrant are those who have a high level of influence on your career, yet with whom you currently have a weak relationship."

Matt interjected: "OK, I've got a couple of questions. First, how should I define 'weak,' and, second, is it for people that have a high influence on my career now, or in the future?"

"Both good questions," smiled Edward. "You remember before when we talked about using your intuition?"

Matt nodded.

"This is one of those situations—*you* define weak. If you feel that your relationship with that person is weak then that means that it is. Only you will know what definitions to place on these relationships. So use your gut instinct. And, second, you are defining people on their *generic* influence on your career—not whether they have influence on it now, but the potential that they have to hold some influence on your career. Both now and in the future."

"OK, thanks, that does make sense."

Edward continued, pointing to the top left-hand quadrant with his pen. "The second quadrant is for the people who have a high level of influence on your career, and who have a strong relationship with you, currently." Matt looked as though he was following Edward's explanation, and so the old man continued.

"In the bottom left-hand corner, we have quadrant three, where we place those people that you have a strong relationship with, but who exert a low level of influence on your career; and in quadrant four are the people with whom you have a weak relationship, but who also have a low level of influence on your career."

Matt was recording Edward's explanations on the paper in front of him.

"OK, got that—so how can I use it?"

Edward laughed. "Golly, you are keen to use it, aren't you?"

"You bet I am!"

"Let's revisit that list that you put together while I was out the back making some tea." Edward gestured toward the list that was a few pages underneath Matt's notes. Matt shuffled his papers so that the two men could focus on this important page together. "What I'm going to ask you to do, is to look at this list that you have put together, and then place people in the quadrant that you think best describes the level of influence that they have on your career, and your current relationship with them."

Edward sat quietly next to Matt while the younger man worked through his list and placed each of the 15 people into the various quadrants within the matrix. He watched, and restrained himself from making any comment. He didn't want to interrupt Matt's thought pattern, and he was also interested to see how well Matt had grasped this whole profile concept.

After about ten minutes, Matt placed the last person into one of the quadrants, and turned to Edward.

"OK—think I'm done."

"Looks good to me—you looked quite decisive about the quadrant that you placed some people in and, for others, you looked like you were thinking about them more carefully—how easy did you find it to allocate people to these quadrants?"

"You're right—some are easier than others. Rich, for example, is someone that I have placed in quadrant one, because he obviously has a high level of influence on my career, but although I think my relationship with him is developing well, there is a way to go before I could place him in quadrant two, I think."

"That's good—you want to be realistic and even conservative when you are going through this exercise—that will give you a more sensible and balanced approach, I find.

"And you listed Jo, your old boss, in quadrant two, I see.

But she's left you now and no longer has any impact on your career?"

"Oh but she does" interjected Matt passionately. "In fact, she's in a stronger position now that she has been promoted. As I have a good relationship with her, if I maintain that relationship, Jo could become an ally for me amongst those higher ranks."

Edward nodded his head, smiling warmly, "Very good, Matt, that's absolutely right. That old phrase 'out of sight, out of mind' has no bearing at all on your career. People who you no longer work with can still influence your career—both positively and negatively. You certainly want to keep them 'warm' in terms of your relationship with them if they move elsewhere in the organization."

"And who's that you've placed in quadrant three? You looked like you were taking some time in positioning them," prompted Edward.

"Yes, that's Tim. He's the guy that got promoted ahead of me early this year. I have a really good relationship with him, but he doesn't have any influence on my career, so I've placed him in quadrant three."

"He doesn't have any influence on your career?" Edward asked the question with a tone that suggested "Are you sure?"

Matt looked again at the matrix in front of him, trying to see whether Tim should fit elsewhere.

Edward prompted him: "Think about it. Now that Tim has been promoted, he will be attending the managers' meetings. They will talk about all nature of things that affect the sales team in those meetings—you may even be discussed, Matt, and Tim would have an opportunity to put forward his point of view about you. Do you want to consider moving him to quadrant two, perhaps?"

Out of sight
shouldn't be out
of mind for
relationships.

"I really hadn't thought of that at all–but you are right. I was completely forgetting the fact that he is included in conversations like that–I should see him in a different light."

"Yes, you should–don't let your ego get in the way of correctly classifying people here. Remember also that you should revisit this matrix often. What you have written down is not set in stone for ever more–you should review it as your situation, and the situations of others, change."

"Yes, that is a good point–I hadn't considered that." Matt made a note of Edward's latest point on the pile of paper in front of him that had become his makeshift notepad.

"Good–so you have a pretty good summary of all the relationships that are most important to you right now. What are you going to do with this information?"

Matt didn't know. He looked at the matrix, looked back at Edward, and shrugged his shoulders.

"What's the point of giving all that thought to this if you aren't going to do anything with it?" Edward asked rhetorically.

He continued. "The reason that we are doing this is to make sure that you are known by the right people–the third and final layer of the profile element. What this exercise has given you is a picture of where your relationships are now. What we need to do is identify which relationships can stay where they are, and which relationships need to be developed so that they have more impact on your career."

"Ah, I see. So we need to take some action now, to make use of this information?" asked Matt.

"That's exactly what we need to do. To make it a little easier for you, there is a specific strategy that you need to consider for each of these four quadrants–so let me share the strategies with you. This time, let's take them in reverse order."

The two men focused once more on the diagram in front of them, now littered with the names of the 15 people that Matt had highlighted earlier.

"Now, quadrant four is straightforward. These people have a low impact on your career, and you also have a weak relationship with them—so, in our context, pay them no attention—they have no influence in terms of your career." Before Matt could say anything, Edward had moved on to the next quadrant.

"Quadrant three—these are the people that you have a great relationship with but who have very little influence on your career. These are what we call in the trade, 'friends'." Edward smiled at Matt with a cheeky glint in his eye. "Friends are just that. Spend time with them just as you do now—but be aware that your relationship with them is highly unlikely to move your career forward in the dramatic ways that you are looking for."

"Isn't that a bit harsh?" Matt asked.

"No, not really" was Edward's stark reply. "You need to focus in on those people who have the potential to impact on your career, Matt. If these people can't do that for you, still spend time with them—in fact, I would guess that you would need to alter very little about the way that you interact with them—but be conscious that having lots of business *friendships* isn't going to drive your career forward."

Though this seemed harsh, Matt could see the logic behind what Edward was saying.

"Don't switch off from these relationships completely though—in terms of networking, they are very valuable to you—and we'll come to that later."

Matt smiled—he was pleased that these relationships could be used constructively for some other benefit.

The matrix, hand-drawn, contains:

- Vertical axis labelled **INFLUENCE**, from **high** (top) to **Low** (bottom)
- Horizontal axis labelled **RELATIONSHIP**, from **Strong** (left) to **Weak** (right)

Top-left quadrant: **MAINTAIN THESE RELATIONSHIPS** — Jo Nigel, Peter, Tim

Top-right quadrant: **NURTURE THESE RELATIONSHIPS** — Rich, William, David

Centre: Above the Line 2 | 1; Below the Line 3 | 4

Bottom-left quadrant: **FRIENDS** — Tom, Jasper, Sam, Ali, Annie

Bottom-right quadrant: **NO INFLUENCE – NO ATTENTION** — Sarah, Tony, Jim

"Now, quadrants one and two are the most important—these are your *above-the-line* relationships," continued Edward.

"What do you mean *above the line*?"

Edward ran his Montblanc along the line at the bottom of the matrix that was marked relationship. "This line is our strategic divide. Everything *above* the line reaps you benefit in terms of your profile. Everything *below* the line doesn't. Career helium comes from those relationships that are positioned above the line." Matt nodded, and made a note—he wanted to remember that.

"Now, in quadrant two are those people who have a strong

Career helium comes from those relationships that are positioned _above_ the relationship line.

influence on your career, and with whom you already have a good relationship. Your strategy for these people is to continue doing what you are doing. You want to maintain the strength of these relationships—so consciously monitor them, and if you haven't seen anyone within this quadrant for a time, think of how you can invigorate that relationship. That might mean meeting them socially, or stopping by their office, calling them up to ask their advice on something, meeting them for a 'catch-up coffee'—whatever is appropriate for the two of you to invigorate or maintain your relationship. The important thing is that you think 'when was the last time I saw this person?' and if it's longer than three months, do something to reconnect with them."

"OK, three months" muttered Matt as he diligently made his notes.

"I find that's a good benchmark, but, again, use your intuition." Matt nodded as he wrote.

"The final quadrant—quadrant one—is the most important for you." Matt looked up from his paper and focused his attention on Edward.

"You have highlighted these people as the individuals who have the highest influence on your career, but with whom you currently have a weak relationship. These are the people that really matter to your future career so you need to have a strategy for developing your relationship with them. You need them to know who you are, and also—and this is most important—that they see you, and what you do, in a positive light. You have listed four people down here, Matt, and you need to consider a strategy for raising their awareness of you. For these people, there are some specific steps that you should take." Edward took another piece of paper. He wrote five questions on the paper in front of him.

1. What contact do you currently have with them?
2. What do you know about them? Think business, think personal.
3. What legitimate opportunities do you have to spend more time with them?
4. What other opportunities might there be for you to spend more time with them?
5. How could *you* be useful to *them*?

"By asking yourself these questions in relation to each of the people you have listed in quadrant one, you will develop a strategy for getting closer to these key people. You will identify the opportunities that already exist—and perhaps that you are not making the best use of—to spend time with that person and get to know them, as well as giving them an opportunity to get to know you and what you do. As you spend time thinking about these questions, the opportunities that you have for developing a closer relationship with each of the people that you have listed in this quadrant will emerge. This may take you a little time as you will need to give it some thought."

Edward gave Matt a moment to process everything he was saying. "Now, don't forget what I like to call the entourage factor. As you are thinking about these questions, consider who you might know that may already have a strong relationship with your target person. Could you use your existing relationship with this individual as a bridge to the person you want to forge a relationship with? This can be powerful—we all take the recommendations of those that we respect very seriously. If you are introduced through someone that your target person already knows, they will pay more attention to you—as you are coming to them as a recommendation."

"I see how that could be powerful. In fact, there are some

Utilize the power of the entourage factor.

people who I have placed in quadrant two that I could use as a bridge to the people that I want to get close to in quadrant one."

Edward smiled at his young friend. "Yes, very good. Utilize the good relationships that you have already in any way you can. We are all connected, so make the most of those connections."

Without warning, Edward turned his attention away from the quadrant diagram that they had both been poring over.

"Do you want to see why I brought you here?" he asked, standing from his chair and kicking a few balloons that were lying around his stool as he got up.

"Definitely! I've been curious ever since we arrived here," replied Matt enthusiastically. Whilst Edward's latest lesson was very interesting for him, the nagging question as to why his mentor had brought him to this rather unusual venue was still at the back of his mind.

Edward picked up a large round silver balloon from one of the boxes next to the workstation.

"Pass me that tube would you?" Edward pointed to a long tube that was fixed to a large tank standing just next to the workstation. Matt took the industrial-looking nozzle in his hand and lifted the tube over to Edward, who was waiting with the empty silver balloon in his hand.

"I brought you here to remind you of something, Matt."

"Really? What's that?"

"Well, often we get so wrapped up in the detail of our lives that we forget the big picture—the reasons why we are doing something. It's very easy to lose sight of that overarching focus. So, I brought you here to remind you of that—I wanted to remind you of the power of career helium, and it seemed appropriate to do that now as we focus on your organizational profile. I wanted to bring you here to give you an experience that was deliberately different, so that it would stick in your mind." Matt was amazed at the knack Edward had of capturing his full attention. During the relatively short time that he had known him, Matt was developing a deep admiration for his mentor as well as a genuine gratitude for sharing his secrets of success with him. Edward was phenomenal—a man perfectly at ease with himself, who had clearly found a recipe that had given him focus, success, confidence, and self-assured inner happiness. Matt had never met anyone as motivating to be around as Edward. He had found his role model—this was who he wanted to be.

Edward inserted the nozzle into the bottom of the silver balloon, and began to inflate it.

"The helium fills this balloon, and transforms it from something lifeless and without form and direction to something that stands proud and confident, and slowly and effortlessly glides toward the ceiling." Edward let the silver balloon escape from his hand. "But you have no ceiling, Matt. Career helium can help you rise as high as you want to. You can achieve anything that you focus your mind on—you just need to identify the opportunities that you need in order to make your dreams a reality. Onward and upward, Matt."

The two men stood for a moment and Matt contemplated Edward's words of motivation and encouragement. That specific phrase felt strangely familiar to Matt, yet he couldn't quite put his finger on why.

Edward broke the momentary silence: "Come with me!"

Before Matt could answer, Edward had disappeared further into the building. Kicking the balloons out of his path as he walked, Matt soon discovered Edward standing amongst huge swathes of material that were suspended from the ceiling, hanging between the wooden beams. Matt held out his hand and touched the material—it had a thick, canvas feel to it and felt slightly rubbery on one side. Looking at the mass of material suspended above him, he realized that it was a hot air balloon.

Whilst Matt was taking a close look at the material, Edward took a pair of scissors, cut a patch of the hot air balloon, and handed it to the younger man.

"I want you to carry this patch with you, Matt. I want you to put it in your pocket every morning and carry it with you as a reminder of the power of career helium. Every time you feel it in your pocket, let it serve as a reminder that if you fill *your* balloon, your career, with career helium, you will rise further than you ever dreamed possible."

"Thank you Edward," replied Matt softly.

He took the patch gently from his friend. "I will remember."

Matt took the patch and placed it in his pocket. He knew that his life would never be the same again.

18

"**Y**ou have a great deal to think about, young man," said Edward as the two made their journey back to the office after their impromptu trip.

Matt was deep in thought, staring out of the window watching the scenery change as they drove through the city. Edward's comment gently jarred him from his dream state.

"What's that? Oh, yes, I do, absolutely. That profiling thing that you have just shown me will be invaluable—I have never thought of relationships in that way before, but now you've shown me that—it all just makes perfect sense. The weird thing is that it all seems so obvious—I can't believe that I've never heard about it before now."

"Well, remember what I said before—people discover it, but because of the fact that it is so powerful, they want to keep it to themselves—which is why people rarely hear about it," replied Edward.

Matt smiled. "I was just thinking a second ago that whilst I need to spend some time putting my profile map together, I've also got that 360-degree thing to do that Rich mentioned just before I left the office—I should get some useful information out of that as well, I would think?" he looked to Edward for confirmation.

"Oh yes—take that seriously—it'll give you another dimension on how others view you. It's likely that most people will have a similar experience of you, and their views will help you to focus on what your unique differentiator is—those unique qualities that describe how you go about doing what you do. You'll need to have a firm grip on what that unique differentiator is for when I take you through the penultimate element of career helium: networking."

"Great, when are you going to teach me about that?" asked Matt enthusiastically.

Just as the taxi was pulling up outside the office, Edward rested his hand on Matt's arm and leant in toward him, as if to emphasize his coming point. "I think you've got enough to be getting on with at the moment, don't you?" he said softly.

Matt smiled in reply. "I guess you're right. Don't run before you can walk, right?"

"Exactly," nodded Edward graciously.

Edward shuffled himself forward on the leather seat as the taxi stopped. "Your turn, I believe," said Edward gesturing toward the cabbie, who was pointing to the fare on the meter in front of him. "Good luck."

Matt turned, reached for his wallet, and before he knew it the taxi door had slammed shut and Edward had disappeared.

Matt climbed out of the taxi himself and, straightening in the midday sunshine, tucked his wallet back inside his trouser pocket. As he did so, his hand brushed against the balloon patch. Matt stopped for a moment and remembered his latest experience with Edward. The memory, a mixture of disbelief and excitement, made him smile as he walked toward the glass door of the office.

The email from HR was waiting for him when he got back to his desk. This meant that Matt could get his 360-degree feedback exercise up and running. He was eager to do that—the sooner he had that information from his colleagues, the sooner he could develop a clear sense of his unique differentiator—and then he could continue his education with Edward. He knew that it was the utilization of all the elements that comprised career helium that would give him the greatest payoff, and he was keen to complete his education and really achieve some results.

"Where've you been?" Tim had wandered over to Matt's desk while he was engrossed in the email.

"Huh?"

"I saw you disappear after the meeting this morning and I've not seen you since—where've you been?" asked Tim.

"Oh, you know, went out to get a coffee and got a bit way-laid—you know how it is. It was such a nice day, I thought I'd get a head start on choosing the people that I am going to ask to provide feedback for me in this 360-degree thing—so sat outside where I could get some peace and quiet." Matt threw in some humor in an attempt to get Tim to change the subject. It worked.

"I know what you mean—when everyone's on the phone in here, you can't hear yourself think," he laughed. "I'll leave you to it—just wanted to make sure everything was OK."

"Oh, everything's great—thanks," Matt smiled, and Tim turned to join his team. He had got halfway when he spun on his heels and walked back toward Matt's desk. He hadn't quite got there when he started speaking.

"Almost forgot to say—Rich wants to see you. He asked me to tell you as you weren't around after the meeting. Don't know what it's about—sorry."

Matt didn't know what it was about either. He hoped that he hadn't got himself into trouble by disappearing off with Edward like that—he intended to use his lunch break to cover the time that he had spent with him, but they spent far more time together than the hour Matt was allowed. Needless to say, he was a little nervous as he went in search of Rich.

Rich had a glass-walled office in the corner of the sales floor. As he wasn't there, Matt left a Post-it note on his screen with a simple message: "Looking for me? Give me a call on ext. 458. Best, Matt E."

Matt made his way back to his desk and clicked on the email from Suzy again. Perhaps now he could get his 360-degree exercise started without any more interruptions. The email explained that Matt needed to select up to ten people that knew him well, and from whom he could solicit honest and confidential feedback on his style and approach at work. He needed to select a cross-section of people—across levels, and from a number of different departments.

He scanned his desk for the notes that he had written whilst he was with Edward in the balloon workshop. Rather than dream up a list of names that he could put forward as his feedback providers, why not utilize the thought, and the names, that he had already put into the profile map? Matt scanned through his notes, and found what he was looking for. He looked over the matrix, and with Edward's explanation fresh in his mind, Matt looked at the names in each of the quadrants in turn. He took a highlighter pen from the top drawer of his desk and highlighted the majority of names within quadrant two, and just one of the three names in quadrant one. He knew that although these people had a significant impact on his career, he needed to get closer to them first before he could go asking them for feedback. If he put in place the strategies that Edward was sharing with him, he could call on these people for this exercise next year. He highlighted the majority of the names that he had previously placed in quadrant three—these were the people that he worked with most closely, and were largely peers. Whilst these people had limited benefit when thinking about his profile, they were people he worked with often, knew him the best, and would be able to give the most detailed feedback on his approach. This feedback was to be most useful for him as he developed his unique differentiator.

Matt surveyed the names that he had highlighted on the matrix in front of him. He made some minor adjustments to the list, adding a name that he hadn't previously considered when he was with Edward, and entered the names into the online 360-degree feedback system that Suzy had included in her email.

Matt gave the names one final look over and sent the message. Done. He sat back in his chair, and pondered. He reflected on how quickly he had got his 360 completed. It had only been announced that morning and yet he had already completed all the information and was eagerly awaiting the results. Edward would have been proud of him, he thought.

His self-congratulatory reflection was cut short as the phone buzzed beside him. The caller ID showed that it was Rich.

"Hey Rich."

"Matt, hi, thanks for the note—do you have a few minutes now?"

"Sure—be right there."

Matt put the phone down and considered what Rich might want to see him about. He was mystified, and made his way gingerly over to Rich's office.

20

Rich was on the phone, and beckoned Matt into his office with a wave of his hand.

Whilst Matt sat across from Rich at his desk he looked around the office. Matt knew this office well from the days when it had belonged to Jo. There were no longer any flowers, no family photographs, except for one that was turned toward Rich and Matt couldn't see. Instead, there were pictures of football teams and motorbikes, along with numerous framed sales awards, some dating back ten years. Matt looked around the office, soaking up the clues about Rich's personality and interests from the memorabilia surrounding him.

Rich finished his phone call. "Sorry about that, Matt, how are you doing?"

"Good, thanks."

"Great—what's your take on the 360 idea that I talked you guys through this morning?"

"Oh fine, I mean—I think it's a great idea. In fact—I've already submitted the names of the people that I'd like to provide feedback for me, so the sooner they can do that, the better. I'm really looking forward to seeing what they come up with."

Rich smiled broadly. "Well, that's great, Matt, I'm really

pleased to hear that you are taking it so seriously. In fact— that's kind of why I wanted to speak with you."

Matt was confused. "Sorry, I'm not following?"

"Well, I didn't know that you had acted on the 360 so quickly—but the fact that you have makes me feel even more comfortable about what I wanted to speak with you about."

"Oh?"

"Yes. I wanted to let you know that we are growing the size of the sales team—you know, in line with the plans that I talked you through when we had lunch, and that means that I have an opening for a Sales Manager."

Rich paused and looked at Matt for some response.

"Oh. OH! Great!"

Rich laughed.

"I thought you might like that! So—obviously, there will be the promotion panel as usual, but I wanted you to know that I was going to put you forward for that. Provided you are interested of course?" he asked, with mock sarcasm.

"Oh, wow, definitely, yes. That's great!"

"Good—that's what I hoped you would say! Now, the only stumbling block is that it won't be immediate—as you know, it's currently the end of our sales year, and a few of the members of the promotion panel are out of the office over the next month or so finalizing deals before the end of the budget year, so the panel won't be for a couple of months. But in some ways that's good, because it allows you extra time for any preparation that you might like to do."

That was exactly what Matt was thinking. He knew some people on the panel but not all of them—so the delay, although unusual, would actually work out well for him. He would be able to invest some time in raising his profile with some of the people on the panel way ahead of the actual promotion meeting itself. He needed to be sure that all his preparation effort was focused on the right audience, though.

"Can you tell me who will be on the promotion panel, Rich?"

"Sure—no problem. I've got the list here so I'll email it over to you later on today."

"Great—and I'd really like to know what the panel will be looking for from me—perhaps I could buy you a coffee later this week and you can give me your view on what I need to concentrate on to make sure that I place myself in the best position?"

"Sure, I'd be happy to help you, Matt."

Rich seemed touched that Matt asked for his help.

"Thanks for the vote of confidence, Rich, I'm really excited about this!"

Rich stood and, smiling, offered Matt his hand. "You are very welcome—I'm enjoying working with you, Matt, and I want you to be successful."

The two men shook hands, and Matt left the office with a distinct spring in his step.

21

On the train home that evening, the enormity of the task in front of him hit Matt. The time and focus that he had invested in building a relationship with Rich, and doing all he could to support him from within the team, was paying off—he had his support. He needed to pay that back and show Rich that he had backed the right horse by performing well at the promotion panel. He was acutely aware that Rich had put his professional relationship at stake by nominating him for the promotion, and that his performance on the panel would not only reflect on him, but also on Rich, and he wanted that to be nothing but a positive outcome for both of them.

He was lucky that there would be a few months' lead time before the actual promotion meeting took place. Just as he had promised, Rich had sent Matt the names of the people who would be sitting on the promotion panel. In fact, many of them were people that Matt had already mapped in quadrant one of his profile matrix—people that had the potential to have a significant impact on his career, but with whom he didn't have a strong relationship with currently. The couple of extra months he had before the date of the panel would work out well for him—he could avoid the "relationship cramming" trap that some of his colleagues had fallen into in the past—

trying to build a relationship too quickly and for too obvious an outcome. Matt had watched that from afar and had always thought that kind of approach transparent and sycophantic, and that really wasn't his style. He needed to get closer to those people, but how?

As the train emptied at one of the large stations that Matt passed through on his journey home, he pulled his notebook from his bag. He flicked back to the original career helium diagram that Edward had drawn for him all those months ago, and he reviewed the two remaining elements that Edward hadn't yet shared with him: *networking* and *politics*. Both were useful, but networking was undoubtedly most useful to him right now. He needed to track down Edward as soon as he could. He needed to network with the people who were to be sitting on the promotion panel, and he needed to start as soon as possible. But how could he find Edward?

It had always struck Matt as a little odd that he had never known how to contact Edward. He had met his mentor purely by chance that first day in Starbucks, and since then had bumped into him just at the moment when he most needed his counsel and guidance. That had never really been a problem, except for those occasions when he really needed Edward's advice and support. This was one of those occasions. Matt was a little agitated by the fact that he didn't have the option just to call up Edward and fix a meeting. However, he had always held a firm belief that things in his life were connected in ways that weren't always known to him and that all things in his life happened for a reason, even if he didn't always know what that reason was. He trusted his instinct, and prayed that Edward would "pop up," in his inimitable style, just when he needed him most. Trying to distract his mind from the fact that time was of the essence in connecting with his mentor, he returned to the location that had become the epicenter of their relationship.

Matt was met with a familiar face.

"Hey Ben—how you doing?" said Matt, greeting Ben the Barista warmly.

"Hey Matt, haven't seen you for a few days, I'm doing good, man. How are you?"

"Good, good. Can I get a tall vanilla latte?"

"Sure can. Hey, you just missed your friend—he was in a few minutes ago."

"My friend?"

"Sure—you know, the older guy, the cool dude with the goatee."

Matt collected his coffee and made his way upstairs, hoping against hope that he would find Edward sitting there waiting for him.

He looked around the tables. Students sat in groups, chatting over mugs that had long gone cold, whilst business people sat alongside them having meetings over impromptu coffees and muffins. Edward was nowhere to be seen.

Matt's heart sank. At least he knew he was in the area—perhaps it was too good to be true to think that Edward would be sitting here waiting for him. What was he thinking? Matt turned around to make his way downstairs. If Edward wasn't here, there was a chance that he was sitting outside somewhere. Long shot or not, it was worth a look, he thought.

"Steady on!"

Just as he turned on his heels, Matt had bumped straight into someone, squashing his paper cup between their two bodies and almost spilling his latte all over them both.

"Oh, I'm so sorry," he said automatically, instinctively checking himself to see the coffee damage. He had escaped without a stain.

"Phew, that was close" he sighed, looking up to make eye contact with the person he had bumped into.

He was greeted with a beaming smile that he recognized, and that couldn't have been more welcome.

"Edward!"

"That was close—this is one of my favorite shirts!" he laughed.

"Oh, I didn't spill any coffee on you, did I?"

"No, no, I'm fine," he said, brushing his shirt and buttoning up his jacket.

"You do look like you are in a bit of a rush, though?"

"Well I am—I mean, I was. Ben mentioned that you might be up here, which was such a stroke of luck as I really need to speak with you. I've got some great news you see, and I really need your help." Edward interrupted his young protégé, laughing.

"OK, OK, well you've found me now, so you can take a deep breath, Matt!"

Matt smiled and did just that—he was genuinely relieved to have bumped into Edward, both literally and metaphorically.

The two men gravitated toward a couple of chairs in the corner of the room, as far from the noisy students as they could.

"So—you have some news?" asked Edward.

"Yes." Matt paused for a moment and composed himself, before he heard himself say his news out loud for the first time.

"Rich has put me forward for promotion."

"Oh, congratulations! That's wonderful, Matt. You must be so pleased."

"I am, I'm really pleased. And it's all down to you, Edward."

"Oh, no, not at all," said Edward shaking his head. "I've just opened your eyes and given you some tools—you're the one that has put them into practice—you've done that yourself. But—not wanting to dampen your enthusiasm—this is just a nomination; you now need to make sure that you demonstrate to Rich that he has made the right decision in nominating you by preparing properly and passing the promotion panel."

Matt smiled. He could always rely on Edward to give him a realistic view, and make sure that he didn't lose sight of reality.

"Yes, absolutely, which is why I wanted to meet up with you—I need to know how to network. You see I'm in quite a fortunate position in terms of the date of the promotion panel. Usually they happen fairly immediately, but for this one, most of the panel aren't available together for a while so I won't be discussed for at least a couple of months. That gives me some extra time beforehand to make sure that I get to know all the people on the panel that I don't already have a relationship with. Funnily enough, those people are mostly the ones that I had already listed in quadrant one of the profile matrix when we met at the balloon shop."

"Yes—funny that, isn't it?" Edward added, with a slight sarcastic tone.

"OK, OK. I know—I'm beginning to see now how all of this fits together, laughed Matt.

"I know—I'm only teasing," Edward added. "The thing you have to remember about career helium is that it's all linked together—and all the elements connect with each other, they complement each other. So you get most benefit and success when you build on one with another—going through the profiling exercise that I took you through in the balloon workshop provides the basis for your networking strategy. As you rightly point out, Matt, once you've identified those people above the line in quadrant one and two that you want to develop, or deepen, a relationship with, you then need the knowledge and strategies of the networking element to enable you to do that effectively."

"Exactly and that's where I am now—and why I am so glad that I ran into you. I want to make the best use of the next couple of months to make sure that I network with the people on the promotion panel I don't know so that I can raise my profile with them. I don't want them saying 'We don't know who he is' like they did the last time."

Edward smiled. "Well in that case, let the lesson, begin!"

Edward removed his Smythson journal from his bag, and laid his beautiful pen on top of it. Somehow, this signaled the beginning of the lesson. Matt mirrored him by doing the same, although his notepad and scruffy pen didn't quite have the elegance or presence of Edward's accoutrements. He reminded himself of the promise that he made himself when he first met Edward, that he would buy himself a Montblanc if he won his promotion. If all went according to plan, that would be little more than a few months away.

"Can I just check that my understanding of networking is the right one?" Matt said, taking the lead in the conversation.

"Go ahead," invited Edward.

"Well—I've always seen it as schmoozing with people, people who can help you get what you want."

Edward laughed.

"That's not an uncommon view," he laughed. "And that's why a number of people aren't comfortable with the concept of networking, and find it very difficult."

"Well I guess people find it difficult because they don't know how to do it, and actually find it more than a little daunting—they don't know what to do. I know I don't," confessed Matt.

"I'd agree with you there, Matt. It's a really important skill in business, and in life as well, actually. It's not difficult, but it can carry some negative connotations with it—particularly when you use like words like 'schmoozing'—that make a lot of people feel uncomfortable about it. Let me try and demystify it a little for you. It's actually quite straightforward if you follow a few simple rules." Edward saw Matt grab his pen. "But we'll get to those shortly."

"First of all, although we'll call it networking, because that's what people label it, I'd like to reposition it in your mind in a slightly different way, which will smooth some of the roughness that you currently associate with it. Try thinking of it more as *connecting* with others." Matt looked a little taken aback. He furrowed his brow.

"What's the difference?" he asked.

"The difference is very small, but important. It alters the way that you view it, and I hope it will help you to approach it with a slightly different, more positive mindset. The way that you approach networking is all-important. People are intuitive, some more than others, and if you are focused on meeting someone in order to get something, then it's likely that they will sense that, and will not be as open to you as they would usually be. Connecting has more of a 'meet someone without an agenda' feel to it. It puts true connection and friendship first, ahead of personal, or business gain. If you remember one thing about networking, remember this: begin a relationship asking 'What can I do for them?' rather than 'What can they do for me?' That in itself turns most people's view of networking on its head, and if you take that approach, you will develop a much more authentic relationship, one that will stand the test of time, and will reap benefits for you both."

Connect rather than network. Ask "What can I do for them?" rather than "What can they do for me?"

"That's certainly a more positive way of approaching it," said Matt, writing Edward's last phrase in his notebook.

"I think so, and it's an approach that has certainly served me well. Many people, particularly in business, meet people and you can just tell that they're trying to work out how they could use that person. I've always found that rather distasteful. People will by nature help those that they feel some affinity and affection for—and you can only get that by putting your agenda aside, and developing relationships in a more authentic way. This authenticity makes the connection. The connection is the foundation for the true relationship." As he spoke, Edward wrote the phrase in his journal.

"I get it. I know just what you mean. I've always thought that business doesn't need to be *business*. If you personalize the way you do things, and share more of your true self with others, you get the same in return. I've always been myself with my own small team—and I think they've always appreciated that."

"Good. Well, sounds like we're on the same page then. You're already halfway to becoming a great networker."

Matt smiled. He had often felt a bit out on a limb by taking this approach. He did things differently to everyone else, and even though this felt natural to him, he had always been made to think by others that somehow he was doing things in the "wrong" way. He was pleased that Edward had vindicated his approach.

"There are a few rules that I've always lived by when I've been networking that have stood me in good stead," said Edward picking up his pen and turning to a clean sheet of paper in his journal. "I think that these will make sense to you, Matt, from what you have told me already. These points will give you an approach that will help you to connect,

Put your agenda aside.
Authenticity makes the
connection. The connection
is the foundation for the
true relationship.

rather than simply network, putting the person and the relationship before the agenda. I call them the 'philosophies of eight'."

"The what?" Matt sounded puzzled.

Edward smiled. "'The philosophies of eight'" he repeated, simultaneously drawing a figure "8" on the page in front of him.

"Think of the figure 8—it's a perfect, symmetrical shape that flows together in a beautiful way. It has no sharp edges, and flows on infinitely. I think that it illustrates the career helium approach to networking perfectly: focus first on the person, rather than the agenda—a longer-term approach that, by definition, has a natural flow to it. The notion of networking that I'm talking about doesn't have the sharpness of the networking that you have experienced—this is more authentic, which gives it a more palatable smoothness."

Matt copied the figure of 8 into his own notebook, and slowly retraced his pen over the graceful number as he listened to Edward's explanation.

"I can see that. A slightly softer approach."

"Softer, yes, I can live with that, but no less focused."

"OK, makes sense. So what are your philosophies of eight?"

Edward smoothed the fresh page in front of him with the palm of his hand, as if preparing it for what was to come. He looked at Matt and smiled. "Ready? Let me share my networking philosophies with you."

Edward took his pen and began to write each of the philosophies on the page in front of him. Matt admired his beautiful handwriting, and wished that he had paid more attention to developing such an artistic style when he was in school. As part of the first generation to grow up studying with computers, his handwriting was spidery and largely unintelligible to anyone except himself. He watched as Edward crafted the first philosophy.

"*We're all in the same boat. None of us can make our dreams come true without the help of other people.*" Edward slowly read the philosophy as he wrote it, and then turned to Matt. "Think about it. There is no one that ever achieved anything without the help and support of others. Learning to walk, raising a family, or creating a business—we all need help. See your networking with others as an opportunity to help *them* achieve something. If you can help, do so, and without expecting to get anything in return. In my experience, if you take that approach, when you need help, it will be forthcoming. We're all in this together, Matt."

Matt nodded. As usual, what Edward was saying made sense to him so he copied down the first philosophy, and added some additional comments just underneath it that paraphrased Edward's explanation . He looked up in anticipation of the second philosophy.

"*Each person you meet is an exercise in connecting.* Don't wait for a formal 'networking' session—every interaction you have with someone new is an opportunity to build a relationship and connect with someone. Always be open to connecting with others—there's no need to get yourself in a 'networking frame of mind.' If you are just being yourself, you will always be open to meeting new people, and seeing where those connections will take you. If you take this approach, you will gather new friends and contacts in the most unexpected of places."

Edward continued: "*Opportunity exists everywhere.* Often if you go looking for something, you can't find it. If you

Networking: The philosophies of eight

1. We're all in the same boat. None of us can make our dreams come true without the help of other people.

2. Each person you meet is an exercise in connecting.

3. Opportunity exists everywhere.

4. Be yourself. Know your unique differentiator. Share it.

5. Assume that each connection you make will blossom into friendship, business or otherwise. Greet them and treat them as you would a friend.

6. Treat your network as you would your garden. Plant it, nurture it, give it time to blossom, and pick it only when it has bloomed.

7. Give. Give. Give. Only then ask.

8. Most people aren't mind readers. They won't know how they can help you unless you tell them.

adopt this idea of always being open to connections, you will get what you are looking for, probably when you are not specifically focused on looking for it." Matt smiled. "That reminds me of my last girlfriend," he laughed as he recounted the story for his friend. "I'd been single for ages and had given up on finding someone, and then when I was doing my shopping in the supermarket one day, and my mind couldn't have been further from the subject of girlfriends. I met the girl who I then dated for over a year!"

"There you go—exactly!" applauded Edward. He liked it when Matt linked his lessons to his real-life experience—it demonstrated to him that Matt understood the premise of what he was talking about.

"Good—so onto philosophy four—*be yourself. Know your unique differentiator. Share it.* This philosophy underpins the authenticity that we've been talking about, Matt. There's no need to have a dual personality—the Matt at home, and the Matt at work. Be who you are, people want to get to know *you*, not the 'you' that you think they want to meet, but the real you. Be yourself." Matt nodded—this matched exactly with his own approach, so Edward's advice was music to his ears.

"Now, that reminds me," continued Edward. "This is where the profile element we were talking about before links to the networking element. You remember that we talked about the importance of knowing what your unique differentiator is? We talked about that in the balloon workshop. Have you given that some more thought?"

"I have indeed given it some thought, and I've got a pretty good idea of what my unique differentiator is, but I want to get the results of the 360-degree feedback exercise that I told you about, so that I can make sure that my idea matches with the views of my peers and colleagues. Does that sound sensible?" Matt asked.

"Sounds very sensible—it's always a very good idea to get some feedback from others just to ratify your own thoughts. You're fortunate that you have had a 360, but you don't always need to do that—just gathering some anecdotal feedback from some trusted colleagues will do the trick. It sounds like you will have your unique differentiator pinned down pretty soon—you'll need that when you start networking, so that you are clear about how you pitch yourself to people."

"Yes—I understand that—I'm comfortable that I have that in hand, I'm almost there."

"Great—so on to philosophy five, then?" continued Edward.

"*Assume that each connection you make will blossom into friendship, business or otherwise. Greet them and treat them as you would a friend.*" Before Edward could offer some additional explanation, Matt interjected.

"OK, I think I get this one—it's about going in there and meeting someone with the mindset that they are a friend already—because you treat people differently who are your friends. Is that right?"

"Yes, that's on the right lines. When people meet for the first time, they are unconsciously judging each other and making snap decisions about each other. You can avoid that and give people a warmer start if you can 'pretend' that you know them already—and warmly greet them in the same way that you would a friend—this starts you off on a great footing."

"Yes, that's what I thought. OK, good." Matt completed his scribbling on his notepad. "Next?"

"Philosophy six: *Treat your network as you would your garden. Plant it, nurture it, give it time to blossom, and pick it only when it's bloomed.*"

"Mmmm, what does that mean?" asked Matt, caught off guard by Edward's unexpected metaphor.

"Well, think about how you tend a garden."

"Gardening isn't one of my top recreational activities, I have to say," said Matt with a cheeky grin.

"I can imagine it's not, but you'll know enough about gardening to be able to relate to this, I guarantee you. What this philosophy is saying is that you need to give your contacts time to get to know you and feel comfortable with you, before they provide any help or support for you. You don't just plant a seed, and expect there to be a flower there the next day—you need to plant it, look in on it from time to time, water it when required and then, in time, and when the conditions are right, the seed will bear you a flower. If you take the same approach with networking—you will reap a similar result. Meet your contact, develop the relationship by calling or meeting them occasionally, perhaps send them an email or an article you've come across that you think may be of interest to them—anything that's appropriate just to nurture your relationship and keep it ticking over. Then, when they see something or hear of something that could be of help or of interest to you they will be more likely to pass it on."

"OK, I see—so it's a little like what my parents used to tell me at Christmas when I was a kid—'it's better to give than to receive'?" asked Matt.

"Similar to that, yes—the principle is about giving to others, and not expecting to receive at that moment, to use your words. If you nurture the relationship properly, you will receive—but at some time in the future."

"There's no expectation there—that's the difference?" offered Matt.

"Exactly. And that neatly leads me to our penultimate philosophy, point seven: *Give. Give. Give. Only then ask.*"

Edward gave Matt a moment to consider the unusual nature of this latest philosophy.

"Right—that's emphasizing the point that we just talked about—help others, with the belief that at some stage in the future, they will help you when you need it?"

"Yes, and also that you need to give the relationship time to develop trust and respect between you before you ask for something that you might need. Asking is fine—but remember that you ask friends for help, and not acquaintances—so make sure that your relationship has developed the trust and respect that are the hallmarks of friendship before you start asking."

"And the last of the philosophies of eight: *Most people aren't mind readers. They won't know how they can help you unless you tell them.*"

"OK—I think that one is pretty clear. Assuming that the trust and respect is there, and it's appropriate for the relationship, tell people how they can help you—don't expect them to read your mind. So, in other words, be explicit."

"That's exactly right," complimented Edward. "Those are the philosophies of eight—if you network using these as your guiding principles, you won't go wrong, my friend."

Matt took a moment to complete his notes, then turned his attention to his mentor.

"There's just one thing that's still puzzling me, Edward," he said.

"Really? What's that, Matt?"

"Well, all this makes sense, but I'm struggling with the fact that I'm really nervous about introducing myself to people—I don't enjoy it, and I don't know what to say. The nature of these philosophies assume that I can do that, and I'm not sure that I can."

Edward smiled. "I know what you mean, I was like that once. Let me see if I can put your mind at rest a little, and make this a bit easier for you."

"Thanks—that would be good," said Matt, clearly relieved.

"Have you ever wondered why you feel like that?" Edward asked, resting his pen in the crease of his journal.

"Not really. I've never really thought about it, to be honest."

"Well, you aren't alone, Matt, a lot of people feel the same way that you do. I don't think I have ever shared this element of career helium with anyone that hasn't recounted a fear of meeting new people. It's often the result of two things. One is that they have a little voice in their head saying things to them like 'Why would they want to meet you?', 'You're nothing special,' and things like that. This negative self-talk is a bit like having a little devil sitting on your shoulder—and you need to consciously counterbalance that by telling yourself the positive truth—that you do have something to add, and that people do want to meet you."

"I know what you mean—but that little voice creeps in, no matter what I try and do."

"It will always be there—but if you develop a strong belief that you do have something to add—which everyone does—then you can use self-talk consciously, and keep telling yourself all the positive things that you have to offer others. This is another reason for clarifying your unique differentiator, Matt. This will give you a tangible and positive focus that you can use as your counterbalancing positive self-talk."

Matt appeared visibly relieved by Edward's explanation—he was certainly familiar with the unconscious negative self-talk that he had described. He had heard that little voice for as long as he could remember.

"And what was the second thing?" asked Matt.

"Let me ask you a question," replied Edward. "Cast your mind back to when you were a little child. Can you remember your parents ever saying to you 'Don't talk to strangers'?"

Matt was a little suspicious. He thought this was an odd question to ask.

"Well, yes, of course, doesn't every parent say that to their child?" he replied, wondering where Edward could possibly go with this slightly obscure line of questioning.

"Yes, they do, and of course it's a very sensible thing to say. In fact, most drum it into their children for at least ten years. The result of this as they move into adulthood, and enter the world of work, is that they have this serious warning ringing in their ears. When it comes to networking, this fuels that little devil that we talked about—because what is networking, essentially?"

Edward paused before continuing: "Networking is essentially talking to strangers! So, it's no wonder that people find it difficult—because it goes against everything that their parents drummed into them as a child!"

Matt burst out laughing. "My goodness—you are absolutely right. I had never considered that. It's no wonder that people find it difficult—they were told for years not to speak to strangers, and networking can mean that you need to actually introduce yourself to these strangers, which is even worse!"

The two men laughed together, so loudly in fact that the two business people sitting a few tables away turned to look at what was causing such hilarity.

"OK, I think I'm cured—that does put my fears into perspective!" chuckled Matt.

"It does give some explanation, doesn't it?" Edward smiled.

"Yes, absolutely!"

"So, you feel more comfortable with the networking element now?" Edward asked, closing his journal and sitting back into his chair.

"I do, thanks. Now all I have to do is to make an appointment to see all the people that are sitting on the promotion panel, and I'm set."

"Yes—you could go down the formal route by making a appointment, or you could utilize the entourage factor."

"Now, you've mentioned that before. Remind me?"

"Sure, this is when you identify someone that you know well who knows the person that you want to raise your profile with—then you ask them to introduce you. The premise is that you will be welcomed more warmly, and given more 'airtime' if you are introduced by someone that the key person respects."

Matt nodded. "Yes, that's right, I remember now."

"So, by all means make appointments with some people, but utilize your existing contacts where you can to engage the entourage factor."

"Good advice—thanks, I will."

"My goodness, is that the time?" Edward exclaimed without warning. Jumping out of his chair, in a surprisingly sprightly manner for an older gentleman, he hurriedly said his goodbyes to Matt and made his way toward the stairs.

Before Matt had a chance to respond, Edward was gone.

24

Matt wasted no time. He had the list of managers that were to sit on his promotion panel, and he worked his way through it, highlighting those people who he had no link with, and then those whom he knew he could get to meet through an existing contact. He had a list of six people to connect with, and he knew that the sooner he initiated contact with them, the better. Although he knew he had to, Matt didn't like the idea of making cold contact with the people on the promotion panel that he didn't have some kind of relationship or link with. He started emailing the PAs of those people that he had to meet without an introduction, but suddenly had a brainwave.

"But I do know someone that knows all these people," he thought to himself. "Jo!" Matt had watched with admiration as Jo had moved steadily through the ranks, which meant that she knew all the people that would be sitting on the promotion panel—in fact she had worked for most of them, and was now one of their peers. It wouldn't be long, Matt thought, before she would be leading that senior team. Time would tell. She had certainly become very well connected.

He picked up the phone immediately and was surprised

when Jo picked up at the other end—he had been expecting voicemail.

"Jo, hi it's Matt."

"Hi Matt how are you doing?" Jo's reply was warm—she was genuinely pleased to hear from her old team member.

"I hear you've been nominated for the next promotion panel—well done, I'm really pleased for you. You see? I told you you would do it! I hear from Rich that you are making real progress since he's taken over. He's really impressed with you," she said.

"Thanks, Jo, that's kind of you—it's always good to get some positive feedback!"

"Absolutely!" came the reply. "Well you know Matt, even though we don't work together any more, I'm still here for you, so if there's anything that I can do to help you prep for your promotion panel, just let me know.

"Well, actually ..."

Matt really felt the power of networking after his call with Jo. All the other panel members clearly held her in high esteem, and freed up diary space so that she could introduce Matt to them. Matt was surprised, and touched, by the fact that even though Jo was very busy, she took time out of her schedule to personally introduce him to each of the members of the panel. Not only was his introduction to each of them smooth, but it also came with Jo's endorsement, which Matt was sure made a difference to how he had been received. Each of the managers gave Matt a warm reception, which in turn gave him the confidence to share with them his background, his unique differentiator, which he had completed following the release of his 360-degree report, and also his aspirations for the future. After all the meetings had taken place, Matt was confident that everyone sitting around the table at the promotion panel would know him, and have an opinion. He was confident that those opinions would be positive, but he was less concerned about that. That was the only factor that was largely out of his control, and he was completely comfortable that there was nothing further that he could do to place himself in a strong position before for the promotion panel met.

Matt reflected on how far he had come. He remembered the last time he had been put forward for the promotion panel, and failed. He was disappointed and, not that he would have admitted it at the time, a little angry that Tim had got the promotion ahead of him. Looking back, he was glad that he hadn't been promoted. In some ways, his not being promoted was actually the best thing that could have happened to him. After their chance meeting, he had learnt so much from Edward that he wouldn't have replaced that experience for anything. He flicked back in his notebook to all the notes he had written during his various meetings with his mentor, and settled on the very first page. He stared at the career helium diagram and smiled. "Five simple elements," he thought to himself.

Collectively, the most powerful formula he had ever come across.

26

The phone on Matt's desk buzzed into life—the caller ID showed that it was one of the guest phones in the reception area. Strange, Matt thought, he didn't have any visitors booked in today. He pulled up his online calendar as he picked up the phone.

"I was wondering whether you wanted to hear about the last piece of the jigsaw?" said the voice.

"Edward?"

"The very same. Well, do you want to hear about the last element? We've only covered the first four you know."

"I know," replied Matt, "there's still Politics to go, right?"

"Absolutely right. Are you ready to go now?"

Matt checked the time—just before 11—and made a snap decision. He had to take this opportunity.

"Sure—I'll be down in a few minutes."

Matt grabbed his notebook and pen from his desk, switched on his voicemail, and made his way down to reception. Edward was waiting for him as planned.

"My, you do look smart!" he exclaimed as soon as Matt came within earshot.

"It's promotion panel day today," he said. "I don't attend, but it just felt right to wear a suit today, somehow."

"Well, clothes do maketh the man," Edward chuckled. Matt smiled. Edward was always so immaculately turned out, he was the personification of that sentiment.

"So, one more element to go, then?" said Matt.

"Yep. Thought a change of scenery would do us good. There's somewhere I want to take you that will help to give you the perspective you need to consider the final element."

Matt wasn't impressed. "Back to the balloon workshop?" he said limply.

"No, not there—somewhere quite different," laughed Edward. "Come on!"

The two men went outside and Matt flagged down a cab. Within moments, it was doing a U-turn in the street and in no time at all, the cab was driving along the Embankment. Matt watched the sights of London blur past him as the cab sped down the road.

"Are you taking me to the Savoy for lunch?" asked Matt expectantly.

"You should be so lucky," laughed Edward. "No, although you will be able to see the Savoy from where we are going."

That was the clue that Matt needed. Judging from the route the cabbie was taking, he had a suspicion, which was confirmed as they drove over Waterloo Bridge and the cab pulled up outside the impressive London Eye.

"C'mon—our flight is booked in five minutes," said Edward as he jumped out of the cab, leaving Matt to settle the fare. Matt had almost got used to the surprises that had become part and parcel of his friendship with Edward, yet was completely mystified as to why he would have brought him along to this iconic structure to complete his education. After stopping for a second to wonder at this modern marvel of engineering, Matt joined Edward, who was waiting for him at the entry platform to the pods.

Before long, the two men had been escorted to their capsule, which crawled slowly along the walkway and gave them just enough time to join the small group of tourists who were already in the pod. The door closed majestically behind them, and Matt could see that the pod was gently beginning its ascent toward the sky.

"Wow—this is amazing, isn't it?"

"It certainly is. This gives you the best views in London, my friend," Edward said proudly. "We're lucky we have a clear day today—you can see for 20 miles."

Matt gently shook his head in disbelief and gazed across the London rooftops, watching as they slowly sunk beneath him.

After a few moments of individual contemplation, Edward joined Matt at the front of the capsule—looking north across the city toward Westminster.

"Ah, the Houses of Parliament," he sighed. "What a beautiful building—I've loved it since I was a child. If only those walls could talk—the stories they could tell," he sighed.

"Yes, I'm sure," replied Matt "It's amazing isn't it—all that history?"

The two men stood in silence for a second, lost in their own thoughts.

"Well, when I got up this morning, I didn't anticipate standing here with you in a capsule hundreds of feet above London, Edward!" said Matt, fishing for some explanation for their latest excursion.

"I dare say you didn't," said Edward, winking at his young friend. "What do you notice about being up here?" he continued.

"Not sure what you mean," replied Matt, throwing his mentor a quizzical look.

"Come on Matt—we're hundreds of feet above London—what do you see?"

Matt was none the wiser. "I see London, I can look over things, get a different perspective on the city, I guess."

"Ah, ha!" exclaimed Edward, jabbing his index finger in Matt's direction. "Exactly."

Matt looked confused.

"Being up here gives you perspective! You may think you know the city well, but from up here you notice things that you have never seen before. The combination of distance, the structure and design of buildings otherwise invisible to you at street level. The surprising detail that this elevated position gives you.

"Sit down, Matt," said Edward, gesturing toward the oval wooden bench in the center of the capsule.

"I don't quite follow you," Matt confessed.

"We need to investigate Politics in order to complete your education, don't we?"

"Yes—that's the fifth and final element to career helium, but what's that got to do with ..."

"Perspective, Matt, perspective. It's the key to the politics that you need to navigate through if you are to make the power of career helium work for you. Allow me to explain."

Edward reached deep into the inside pocket of his cream trench coat, and retrieved his Smythson journal, which had rolled gently at the edges from the contours of his coat. The old man smoothed the burgundy cover until it regained its usual elegance.

"Now, I guess you've had some experience of the perils of organizational politics, Matt?" Edward asked.

"Well, yes, but to be honest I don't really like getting involved in that kind of thing, so I tend to avoid it."

Edward gently chuckled, suggesting that he seemed to find this amusing. "Oh, my dear boy, you can try all you like, but there is no escape! Politics is omnipresent."

"Omni-what?"

"Omnipresent. It's there all the time, an echo of every action that you, and all your colleagues, take. There's no getting away from it, I'm afraid. You're involved, whether you like it or not. The trick is to know how politics works, so you can make more educated and strategic decisions about how you interact with it." Edward had Matt's full attention.

"How am *I* involved?"

"Well, politics is created by those around you by their actions, their behavior, their communication. Pretending it isn't there still involves you, but in a more passive way. By acting passively you are abdicating your rights to exert your point of view, and giving others an advantage over both you and your position within the organization."

"I don't like the sound of that," said Matt.

"Quite—the worst thing that you can do is carry on regardless, blindly believing that you can be successful without indulging in political play. You will not be successful, Matt, if you do not play a part, no matter how small, in the political landscape at work. Like it or not, politics is a fact of life." Edward's tone was firm.

"OK, I'm sold. So how do I play my part in politics?"

"We'll get to that. The first stage is to understand what drives the existence of politics in organizations. Essentially there are three things—relationships, power and influence, and agenda."

"OK," said Matt, nervously. This really was new territory for him.

You will not be successful if you do not play a part, no matter how small, in the political landscape at work.

"Allow me to explain," continued Edward. "At the core of why people are driven to act in a political manner is their own personal agenda. This could be an agenda that is linked to a business objective, but it's essentially the outcome, the end result that they want to achieve. Their drive to achieve this end result drives their political behavior. Does that make sense?" Edward wanted to check that his young friend was following his argument. He wanted to make sure he could continue. Matt nodded.

"The second is the level of power and influence that some-one has. The greater the level of power and influence they have within any given situation, the more political clout they wield, and the more people will take note of their views and actions. Be aware, though, that someone's power and influ-ence will depend greatly on their *perceived* position within that group. So, whilst someone may have significant power and influence within one area of the organization, that may not mean that they command the same amount of impact in another."

"Yes, I understand. That makes sense."

"The third driver is relationships. Very closely linked to power and influence—the political player relies on the quality of his relationships in order to use his power and influence to drive his agenda forward. It's difficult to achieve this alone, and so he will draw on his previous investment in a strategic relationship in order to gain support for his political agenda."

"All sounds very devious."

"I can understand why you would say that—but think about it. Think about when you were a child. Did you ever play one parent off against the other? You know, you would go and ask your mother for something, and then go and play her answer off against your father?"

What drives politics at work?

- Personal agenda
- Power and influence
- Relationships

Matt flashed Edward an embarrassed smile.

"Sure you did, and all that was happening there was that you wanted something—you had an agenda—and then you used the influence that you had developed through your relationships with both of your parents to get what you wanted. So, really, it's a natural process—we've always done it. Except now, as adults, our behavior is a little more thought through, a little more strategic."

Matt pondered Edward's example from his childhood for a moment. His mentor was right. The politics that he had experienced at work were just an exaggerated and more elegant mutation of the behavior that had come naturally to him as a child.

"Mmmm, you're onto something there, Edward," pondered Matt. He was coming around to Edward's point of view, but he wanted more explanation.

"OK, so say all that's true, what can I do to get involved, and manage the politics that's going on around me, but in a positive way?" asked Matt.

"Now, that's the key, isn't it? The *positive* way," emphasized Edward.

"Most people see politics as a dirty word, but actually it's perfectly natural, and it's not something that's isolated just to the workplace either—you find it in the playground, at home, everywhere. Taking a positive approach, and working *with* it, rather than against it, makes politics less threatening. It becomes just another obstacle to be managed."

"So how *can* I manage it?" asked Matt. He knew that really successful people took politics in their stride, and whilst this was unknown territory for him, he knew that if he learnt and implemented this skill in the same way that he had the others that Edward had shared with him, he would be assured success.

Edward picked up on Matt's tone—a mixture of frustration and disbelief. "Well, it may be more manageable than you think," he said suggestively.

As Edward got up from the bench, Matt realized that their capsule was just approaching the walkway at ground level—he was so engrossed in his mentor's latest lesson that he had completely missed the second half of the Eye's rotation. Edward beckoned to Matt as he stepped out of the pod and walked toward the piazza at ground level.

"Fancy an ice cream?"

Matt snatched a quick look at his watch. He was conscious of the time that he had been away from the office, but wanted more than anything to complete his latest, and final, lesson with Edward. He rolled his eyes.

"Sure—why not," he sighed, giving in to both Edward's persuasive charm and his own desire to learn more about this important subject. With a smile he joined Edward at the ice cream stall that had been set up in the piazza.

"Go on then—what do you fancy?" asked Matt, with the same indulgent tone that a father would use when treating his child.

"Oh, well in that case—it's got to be double chocolate fudge!" exaggerated Edward. Matt couldn't help but smile and gave his order to the ice cream vendor.

"Here you go," he said, handing an ice cream to Edward whilst trying not to drop his own ice cream cone or his change, both of which were in the same hand.

"Oooh, delicious," cooed Edward. "Haven't had one of these for ages." He took a large lick, "Yum!"

"So—you were going to tell me about managing politics,"

said Matt in an effort to get his mentor back on track and complete his lesson.

"Oh, yes, that's right" said Edward, taking another generous lick. "Shall we take a walk in the gardens?"

"Sure," said Matt, deliberately keeping his response short in an effort not to give Edward any opportunity to deviate from the discussion in hand.

"Politics is at work everywhere—can't be avoided, so we just have to live with it. We've established that, right?" continued Edward.

"Yep."

"Right—so the next thing to consider is how to manage that. Now, you can of course become a real politics player, and take an active, almost leading role. Most people, though, don't want to get involved in politics. They see it as something dirty, an unnecessary distraction from 'getting on with the job.' So, what I'm going to share with you is the way that I have always managed politics at work. Not *played* it, but *managed* it, and in a positive, rather than a manipulative way. And that's a concept that people don't usually associate with organizational politics."

"That's exactly what I want to do," added Matt. "I don't really want to get involved, you know, in terms of creating politics—I just want to be able to navigate myself around it, so that I don't get taken advantage of, as you said earlier, and I can always make sure that I'm fairly represented."

"Exactly. Well, you certainly aren't alone there. Now, over the years, I've developed some principles that have enabled me to manage the politics that have been at play around me, and indeed, have touched me, from time to time." Edward began crunching on his cone. "It's worked for me, and I've finessed them over the years, of course. They're very simple-

Manage politics
without going out
of your mind.

- Be aware.
- Keep a sense of perspective.
- Don't take things personally.
- Don't let gravity issues get
  to you.
- Control your impulse.
- Be ethical.

I don't believe in making things unnecessarily complicated. Let me share them with you—the secrets of how to manage politics without going out of your mind." Matt smiled.

"First of all—*be aware.*" Edward paused for a second to emphasize these few words. "Simple, I know, but many people just carry on blindly, not watching what's going around them. What I mean is this: watch the way people interact. How do key people get on with each other? Are there more private meetings going on amongst those people than usual? How do people speak about others publicly and privately? Just being conscious of things such as this is the first step— just being aware of your environment and watching what goes on around you."

"I don't need to do anything, then, just watch?" questioned Matt, sounding a little confused.

"Right—it's just about watching what is going on around you. If you do this you will be able to see, or sense, when that environment is changing, and realize that something might be brewing. Let that intuition that we've talked about before kick in—trust yourself. These changes in behavior, and the usual patterns of interaction that you observe around you, may be an example of someone influencing others in order to drive his or her agenda forward. Remember the drivers that we talked about earlier?"

"Sure—I remember that. So it's just about opening your eyes to what's in front of you, rather than just getting through your day in autopilot mode?"

"You've got it—that's a good description. It's exactly that."

"OK, what's next?"

"Well, the second principle that I've lived by is to *keep a sense of perspective*—and that's why I've brought you here, if you remember."

Matt nodded. "Yes, that was interesting—just the fact that if you look at something—like the city of London—from a different angle or perspective you get to see it in a completely different way. And it's amazing just how different it looks, as well."

"Yes it is—I've always thought it important to, first of all, keep a sense of perspective when living or working in a political environment—you know, just keep a tab on what's really important; and, second, to take a moment out to consider the perspective of others."

"I don't understand that—what do you mean?"

"Have you ever heard the old phrase 'never judge a man until you have walked a mile in his shoes'?" Edward asked.

"Sure."

"Well that's exactly what I'm talking about here when I talk about looking at a situation from another person's perspective. Try to get an insight into what other people's agendas might be that are driving their behavior. Think about the situation from their perspective. Try to imagine what the situation might be like for them, how they see the world, by 'walking a mile in their shoes.' It's a great skill to be able to remove yourself from your own perspective and place yourself in someone else's position to try and view the world from their angle."

Matt nodded. "I get that—it's a difficult thing to do, because normally we are so entrenched in our own worlds."

"Quite—it does you good to leave your world behind sometimes and look at things from someone else's perspective. You'll probably see the situation in quite a different way. If you understand their perspective, that will help you to understand why they acted in a certain way.

"OK, next is something that sounds very simple, but a

Gravity issues: work around them and get on with your life.

great many people feel is very difficult to do in practice: *Don't take things personally.*"

Matt smiled and looked at the floor. "You don't need to tell me about that, I've encountered that problem myself on many occasions!"

"I bet you have—show me someone that hasn't. Most people will have an element of emotional engagement with their work—in other words, they will care about it. So, because of this emotional connection that people make, it's very difficult to let go if decisions are made that you may not agree with. People behave in many different ways on these occasions, and can become very irrational. The way to avoid this is to care about your work and your contribution at work, but to remain realistic about it."

"To keep some sense of perspective?" interjected Matt.

"Yes—there's that word again. That's exactly it. Just remember what's important in life: is the fact that the report you have been working on has been canceled that important? In the big scheme of things, not really."

"Get a life!" exclaimed Matt.

"Yes, but that is an extreme way of looking at it. I'm not saying 'don't care'—as caring is essential to doing a good job—but just retain some sense of reality; don't take things that are largely beyond your control too personally." Edward placed a labored emphasis on the phrase "beyond your control," which wasn't lost on Matt.

"That's really helpful actually—I can relate to that, Edward."

"Look at it this way," continued Edward. "I have a name for those things that are out of your control: *gravity issues. Gravity is something that we all just have to live with and work around—we don't worry ourselves about it. If something happens that's beyond your control, then, sure, feel the frustration, but don't let it upset you. It's a gravity issue—work around it and get on with your life."*

"Gravity issue? Mmmm, I'll remember that," mused Matt.

"Good. I think you'll find the next one of my philosophies useful as well: *control your impulse*." Again, he gave his protégé a moment to digest this notion.

"I think this one largely speaks for itself," added Edward. "If you take things personally, you will find that you naturally react on your impulses because you feel closer to things. In fact you should give even more thought to your responses and actions in a situation that may have a political edge to it. So, acting on your impulses could often be the worst thing you could do." Matt nodded—he could relate to this personally.

"On those occasions where you feel you are operating in a political environment, it's very important to think carefully before responding or acting. Always consider the *consequence* of what you are thinking of saying or doing. What could potentially happen as a result of your action? If there is a risk that you will not be viewed well as a result, then often it's better to say *nothing* than to let your impulses speak for you. I won't deny that it's difficult to do, but take more time to think before you speak or act," Edward said with sincerity.

"That is good advice. There's something to be said for having a professional distance."

"Absolutely—it's just about being realistic, and just accepting that you are operating in a constantly changing environment."

Edward continued: "Now, the fifth philosophy is my personal favorite. You could live your life using this one philosophy, and you won't go far wrong, my friend."

Matt was intrigued. "That's quite a build-up. What is it?" he asked.

"It's quite simple: *be ethical.*"

"That was short and sweet!"

"Well, there's a lot to be said for simplicity! I've always found that the best way to treat people is to be ethical—do the right thing. That's not always the *easiest* thing, but it usually proves to be the best strategy in the long term. You reap what you sow, like attracts like, and all that. If you take that approach, then you will find that you will become less embroiled in politics by definition. Where's the space for Machiavellian politics if you are honest, transparent and ethical?"

"Mmmm, I can see where you're going with that—that's something my parents always taught me, but somehow the message gets blurred along the way."

Edward smiled. "Yes, but there's no reason why you can't reclaim that philosophy," he said with a thought-provoking tone. Matt smiled: "Yes, you're right.

"So these philosophies. How should I make the best of them?"

"Well—think of them as your map, your guiding light. If you follow these philosophies you will find that you are able to work with the politics that emerges from time to time in a much more mature, measured, and effective way. It'll make politics at work easier to manage and less threatening, particularly now that you understand where politics comes from."

"When you first explained to me, all those months ago, that managing politics at work was a key part of using the elements of career helium, Edward, I have to say that this was the part that I was most, I don't know, wary of, I guess."

"Really?" asked Edward. This certainly wasn't the first time he had heard this from one of his protégés, but he was always interested to hear the different perspectives that people had about this important area.

"Yeah, well it's just that people talk about it in such a negative way. And I've never known how to deal with it, so I've done my best to avoid it."

Edward smiled. "Yes, I know what you mean. People do have a problem getting their heads around it, largely because they intrinsically see it as something negative, and potentially overwhelming. What I've given you are some tips on how to work with politics—these are things that have worked for me in the past. They'll prove to be a good start for you, Matt, but essentially you need to find your own way. Over time, I've no doubt that you will add to the philosophies that I have shared with you here—and, in fact, I would encourage you to do that."

Matt smiled. "Thanks Edward—that's valuable advice," he said, gently touching Edward on the arm, emphasizing his gratitude.

"My pleasure," replied the older man, winking at his young protégé.

"**M**att, have you got a moment?"

Matt was concentrating on a detailed spreadsheet when he heard the voice to his side. He was so focused on his PC screen that he hadn't noticed anyone approach his desk. It was Rich.

"Hi, Rich. Er—sure."

He followed his boss into his office, where Rich waited until he had sat down to take his own place behind his desk.

"You know that the promotion panel met today?" he asked.

"Uh-huh."

"Well, I've got some news for you." Rich was deadpan—Matt wasn't able to read him at all. Had he failed his promotion panel for the second time? His heart was in his mouth, waiting for Rich to continue.

"The panel thought that you still have some development areas."

Matt looked to the floor. He had worked so hard ever since the last panel to put the power of career helium into place. He realized that it was still early days for him, but he had already made strides forward—surely that hadn't gone unnoticed?

Rich continued. "But, they also recognized that there had

been a tremendous improvement in your approach to your work since the last promotion panel." Rich finally broke a smile. "They were impressed that since the last time when no one on the panel knew of you or your achievements, that there had been a complete turnaround, with everyone speaking positively about you. Your sales figures are good, your team speak highly of you, and the panel have made the decision that you are ready for promotion, Matt. Congratulations."

With that Rich stood up from behind his desk, and with a broad smile, extended his hand toward Matt, inviting a congratulatory handshake.

"Well done, Matt, I'm really delighted for you."

The two men shook hands warmly, and Matt thanked Rich for his support.

"You're welcome, but you do deserve it. You've shown you've got great potential to do well here." Matt could hardly contain his joy. This was exactly what he wanted to hear. He had learnt a great deal over the past few months, both from Edward and from observing Jo and Rich, and this was recognition that his new approach to work was reaping rewards for him.

Matt left the office with a beaming smile. He felt like he was going to burst—he could hardly contain his joy and excitement. He walked briskly out of Rich's office and instead of returning to his desk, he made his way around the corner into the emergency stairway, which he knew would be deserted as always.

Matt waited until he heard the echo of the door closing behind him, confirming that he was alone on the empty stairway.

"Yeeesssss!"

28

After Matt had reveled in the warm congratulations from his team, and phoned his mother to tell her his good news, there was only one other person that remained on his "can't wait to tell" list. And he knew just where to find him.

Although Edward seemed to be notoriously difficult to track down whenever Matt needed him the most, on this occasion, he was exactly where Matt expected him to be.

"Don't you ever work?" Matt joked as he walked up to Edward, who was sitting in the bay window at Starbucks cradling a large mug in his hands as he watched the world go by.

Edward smiled mischievously. "Well, I must say, you do look pleased with yourself!"

"I am!" Matt deliberately left a moment's silence, hoping that this would accentuate the impact of his next statement.

"I got it!"

Edward beamed and stood up from his chair.

"Oh, well done, Matt, that's marvelous news!" He took Matt's hand, but the handshake turned into an affectionate bear hug. Edward loved these moments: when his protégés reaped success from the secrets he had shared with them. Matt patted Edward on the back with genuine affection—he was indebted to his mentor for introducing him to the powerful secrets of career helium.

"I'm so pleased, I can't tell you," said Matt, shaking his head and smiling. "It's all down to you—you have opened my eyes to a way of working that I would never have discovered on my own. I can't thank you enough for your guidance, mentorship, and most of all, your friendship." His eyes misted over—he felt genuine affection for this man that had taken him on such a journey.

Edward smiled. He was genuinely touched at Matt's display of affection. "You do deserve it. You've been a model pupil—you've listened to advice and, most importantly, you've acted on it. You've taken great steps in making career helium really work for you, Matt."

Edward gestured toward the velvet chair next to him. "Sit down, I've got something for you."

Matt looked puzzled. Edward had given him so much already.

Edward reached into his jacket pocket, pulled out a long black box, and laid it gently on the table. As the sunlight streamed through the window, Matt thought that he could see the indentation of a familiar logo on the box.

He turned to Edward with a look of embarrassed disbelief. "This is for me?"

He took the box and slowly snapped it open. Inside, nestling in black satin was a beautiful, black Montblanc pen. Matt looked back at Edward in disbelief and took the pen gently from the box, holding it reverently in his hands.

"Oh, Edward, I can't. You have given me enough."

"I'd like you to have it, Matt. I know how you have admired my pen, and I want you to have a permanent reminder of the time we have shared, and the secrets that I have imparted to you. Career helium will work for you for ever, and will take you wherever you want to go in your career. I want you to think of that every time you use this pen. It's a symbol of our friendship, our journey, and a reminder that *you* hold the power of career helium in your hand everyday."

Matt was speechless. He had indeed admired Edward's sleek black pen since the first time that he saw it. Matt was touched: the gift was generous and unexpected.

"Thank you for everything, Edward."

"It's been my pleasure, Matt," replied his mentor, gently.

Edward drained his coffee cup. "Well, time for me to be off."

Edward caught Matt off guard somewhat. "Oh, can't you stay awhile?"

"Afraid not—this is where the lesson ends, my friend. The rest is up to you," said Edward standing up.

"You're making this sound like goodbye?" said Matt, sounding worried.

"I'd like to think of it more as *au revoir*," replied Edward, winking.

"I still don't have your number. I don't know how to contact you," said Matt, with a hint of desperation in his voice.

"You've found me whenever you've needed me up to now." Edward winked in response.

There was a finality in Edward's tone of voice. The two men stood in silence for a second, until Edward broke the ice by opening his arms and inviting Matt into a hug.

"Goodbye Matt, and good luck."

Matt watched Edward as he disappeared through the doorway.

Matt's first management meeting. He had sat and watched as Tim and the others disappear to the 10th-floor boardroom every Wednesday at 3 PM for as long as he could remember, and always wondered what was discussed. Now he was about to find out.

Matt wanted his first meeting to go smoothly, and so had prepared a file containing all the paperwork that he thought was relevant, and made some additional notes with his beautiful pen, which still made him smile every time he used it.

Matt had never been to the 10th floor before, and as he stepped out of the lift, he immediately noticed the thicker carpet beneath his feet. Although this was a modern building, the walls had been covered with wooden paneling, giving the floor a much older and more distinguished feel than the rest of the building. This professional and slightly indulgent environment made Matt feel like he had really arrived.

Knowing that the meeting was starting shortly, he hurried down the corridor toward the boardroom. He took a passing glance at the original art on the walls as he passed, wishing he had more time to stop and take a look—he was sure that he saw a Picasso. Turning the corner, he hurried past three large portraits hanging on the wall. He had already passed them when something told him to backtrack—something had caught his eye. Matt took a few steps backward and stood in front of the three large photographs. Each was framed ornately, with a small plaque underneath.

Matt scanned the three pictures until his eyes rested on the one furthest to the right. It was Edward! Matt was taken aback—he had never asked Edward what he did, it had never seemed relevant. Seeing his mentor's photograph displayed so prominently on the wall made him smile. He felt proud that he knew someone of such high standing within the company. He bent a little to read the plaque that sat underneath Edward's picture: "Edward Evans, Chairman. A man devoted to building on his family's legacy—he inspired greatness in all he met." Matt smiled—he certainly recognized this in his friend. He continued to read. "Edward was best known for his philanthropic work, particularly his devotion to the development of young talent within his organization." Matt's smile broadened as he realized that he was one of these "young talents." How honored he was, he thought, that someone so senior would spend so much time developing and mentoring him.

As he continued to read, Matt's eyes widened with disbelief when he saw the years recorded at the bottom of the plaque. Edward had died three years previously. How could this be true? Matt stepped back from the picture and looked intently at Edward's face. He stood for a moment, deep in thought, oblivious to his surroundings.

Memories of his relationship with Edward flickered across his mind's eye. The dream he had long since forgotten of the elevator crashing through the glass ceiling. The nagging feeling that he had met Edward somewhere before. The fact that Edward could never be contacted, that he simply "appeared" when he was needed. The bizarre building filled with balloons that sat surreally in central London, seemingly invisible to everyone but Edward.

Matt shook himself from his thoughts. He looked at Edward's image in the picture and smiled to himself, stroking the piece of balloon fabric in his trouser pocket, and reminding himself of the wonderful and powerful secrets that he had learnt from this great man.

Aware that he was running late, Matt collected his thoughts and walked confidently toward the door of the boardroom.

He opened the door to a standing ovation from his colleagues at the meeting. Matt smiled and joined the meeting, the door closing softly behind him.

Acknowledgements

I have been truly blessed with friends and colleagues who have given me incredible support and encouragement during the writing of this book. Special thanks go to Nigel & Debbie Brown, Richard Cleverly, Alexandra (my NB), Sally Atkinson, and John Drysdale for helping me make important steps forward in pulling it all together. Rick Allen and Joanne & David Tierney not only gave me their time to read the manuscript, but also their honest feedback, for which I am eternally grateful. Renata Wallace gave me space to think, and her unique, approach to business continues to inspire me. David Perry and Barbara Turner, for their blessing, and their discretion in keeping my secret for so long; and also to Jonathan Booth, Rob Parsons, Peter Cox, and Sue Knight for giving me sound advice along the way. I am also so grateful to my endorsers, who have been happy to put their support on paper!

Neil Hoskings gave me the opportunity which took my life in a direction that I could never have imagined. I am indebted to him for opening my eyes to a whole new world, and providing me with the best role model a man could wish for.

I landed on my feet with my publishers, Cyan. None of this would have been possible without the belief of my publisher – Martin Liu. His colleagues have made my first foray into publishing nothing short of a pleasure: Pom, Janey, and Chris, a sincere thank you for your support and dedication.

Matthew & Lewis deserve a special mention. Not least of which for making sure that I am never without raisin bar when I'm round at their house.

Mum – thanks for all the sacrifices you made to make sure that I had the best start. I appreciate everything you have done for me.

And Dax, you have enriched my life more than I can put into words.

And finally, to my readers. Thank you for buying this book, I wish you every success.

David Thompson has worked in the field of people development for over 15 years, holding positions within organizations such as Sainsbury's, Canon, Morgan Stanley, Merrill Lynch and, most recently, as Head of People & Organization Development for ABN AMRO, the global investment bank.

In addition to this, David also speaks publicly on the subject of talent management and career development. He has also been the teambuilding expert on Channel 4's *Big Brother's Little Brother.*

He invites readers to visit his website at *www.careerhelium.com.*